Robert De Niro

Robert De Niro

The Hero Behind the Masks

Keith McKay

Packaged by
Ultra Communications, Inc.

St. Martin's Press / *New York*

ROBERT DE NIRO. Copyright © 1986 by Ultra Communications, Inc. All rights reserved. Printed in the United States of America. No part of this book may be used or reproduced in any manner whatsoever without written permission except in the case of brief quotations embodied in critical articles or reviews. For information, address St. Martin's Press, 175 Fifth Avenue, New York, N.Y. 10010.

Design by Laura Hough

Library of Congress Cataloging in Publication Data

McKay, Keith.
    Robert De Niro, the hero behind the masks.

    1. De Niro, Robert.   2. Moving-picture actors and actresses—United States—Biography.   I. Title.
PN2287.D37M3   1986   791.43′028′0924   [B]   85–25181
ISBN 0–312–68706–0

First Edition
10 9 8 7 6 5 4 3 2 1

To Eva McKay

Contents

Acknowledgments

First and foremost, an unending, heartfelt Grand Canyon of gratitude to Larry Burke and Senior Partner for processing all the words herein. Special, warm thanks also to Berta Walker at the Graham Gallery in Manhattan; to Steve Ruskin at Films Inc., for private viewings; and to Bob Schartoff and Deborah Herschaft at Sterling's Magazines, Inc., for allowing me to rummage through their clippings file. Thanks also to Henry Lipput and Tony Paulazzo for their learned contributions, and to the helpful staff of the Billy Rose Collection at the Lincoln Center Library for the Performing Arts, and Connie Berman and Roseann Hirsch at Ultra Communications, Inc.

I

Formations

On a chilly autumn night in New York City, an East Village movie house that is well known for its midnight showings of contemporary classics is slowly filling up. The crowd is mostly male and appropriately "East Village" in attire—except for two young men down in front. Unlike their frocked and studiously unkempt contemporaries, they are decidedly austere in non-autumn garb: lightweight tan cotton jackets with zippers, T-shirts, and chinos. With their hair close-cut, they have an almost military air. Their conversation is clipped, nearly argumentative in tone, and they sit on opposite sides of an empty seat.

As the theater fills up and showtime approaches, the blaring percussive music coming from the house PA system stops, and a familiar voice-over provides ambience for last-minute arrivals. In perfect sync with that truculent, disembodied voice, one of the pair down in front chimes in: "Are you talkin' to me? Hey! You talkin' to me?? I know you must be talkin' to me. . . ."

A couple of famous lines—totally improvised at the time of their utterance by Robert De Niro in *Taxi Driver*. But tonight's showing at the St. Mark's Cinema is *Mean Streets*, the film that, in a way, started it all. It paved the way for other De Niro characterizations and other collaborations with his *fratello* in spirit, director Martin Scorsese.

Both films have at least two common denominators: a jagged expressionistic vision of New York City's underbelly by night, and Robert De Niro—two-time Oscar-winner, and, already at forty-two, a reclusive legend.

The streets of New York can be a cruel, dangerous, and fickle finishing school. At any moment you could fall between the cracks or get swept aside by the random intrusions of catastrophe, assault, and bad luck. And yet, the labyrinthine city streets form a well-known breeding ground for artist, poet, cabbie, comedian, actor, dreamer, and overachiever alike. Robert De Niro, born on August 17, 1943, is a product of New York's winding streets.

De Niro spent his boyhood in Greenwich Village and the Lower East Side. The rough-and-tumble streets of Little Italy rolled a cautious die in his formation (as a kid he once hung out with a gang) and, of course, years later, on celluloid he would pay homage to those streets, in *Mean Streets, The Godfather, Part II,* and *Once Upon a Time in America*.

In Little Italy the young De Niro was known as "Bobby Milk" because he was thin and as pale as milk. His shyness often kept him from playing with other kids, whom he would watch from across the street. In later years, a friend recalls, "You never saw Bobby without a paperback book under his arm. You'd go to his house on Fourteenth Street and there'd be a zillion hats around, all kinds of costumes."

Young De Niro came of age in a household bustling with the trappings of New York City's burgeoning postwar art scene. Indeed, his life's canvas saw the influence of two masters' strokes.

Robert De Niro, Sr., is an Abstract Expressionist painter and sculptor; he is also a poet. The actor's mother, Virginia Admiral, is also an artist. In fact, once when the young De Niro was hitchhiking around Europe, his peregrinations brought him to Italy. There, in Peggy Guggenheim's Venetian Collection, he saw his mother's paintings on display. "Bobby . . . had no idea he would see his mother's work when he went to Venice," his father has said. "He was particularly proud that his mother had made a breakthrough for recognition that eludes so many women."

"Virginia was the only painter I knew at that time to sell a painting to the Museum of Modern Art," artist Nell Blaine recalls. Both Virginia Admiral and Robert De Niro, Sr., were considered among the most talented and gifted students of the celebrated painter Hans Hoffman, in whose Provincetown, Massachusetts, art class they met in the late thirties. "We talked about them with great respect. They left an aura at the school, where people were either geniuses or nothing," Blaine says. Virginia Admiral, in those "P-town" days, also edited a literary journal called the *Experimental Review*, which published works by the then-unknown Henry Miller, Kenneth Patchen, Laurence Durrell, and Anaïs Nin. DeNiro, Sr., has recalled that one summer in Provincetown, while he was working in a fishery, "I was living with Virginia then and having a hard time with money. Anaïs Nin suggested I write some pornography at one dollar a page . . . it was very hard work, so eventually I went back to the fishery."

In Manhattan, the De Niros' Bleecker Street apartment was always the scene of fascinating talk. "Our standards were so pure, we treated with scorn any humdrum references to the personal. . . . Concepts, ideas were exchanged. Anything less was a tasteless distraction," a friend remembers.

Robert and Virginia broke up shortly after Bobby was born. Virginia Admiral moved to West Fourteenth Street with Bobby, where she started a typing and offset printing service. She has resumed painting but is not interested in talking about the past. "I want to keep my life *my* life," she says.

It has been said that the elder De Niro has always been fiercely independent and that in his earlier years he often put his art before his material welfare. "The main weakness of young painters is a lack of dedication," he has said. "They will stick to art as long as it doesn't cost them anything . . . they must learn to stick with it no matter what the cost." In his lifetime, he has lived on a coal barge and in a tent, and once worked as a waiter in a Greenwich Village dive called The Beggar's Bar. It was there that he became friendly with another young waiter named Tennessee Williams. In 1951, he moved to France, where he stayed for four years, "living in places I could afford, including a house on a mountaintop above a little village called Luchon."

The art world has done very well by Robert De Niro, Sr. He has been the subject of countless one-man exhibitions throughout the United States, and his paintings appear in museums and public collections, including the Metropolitan Museum in New York, the Mint Museum in Charlotte, North Carolina, and the Joseph H. Hirshhorn Museum and Sculpture Garden in Washington, D.C. He first exhibited in 1948 in Peggy Guggenheim's Art of This Century gallery, with Jackson Pollock, Mark Rothko, and other major figures in American Abstract Expressionism. A painter of nudes, still lifes, and landscapes, De Niro has been called an American Fauve. His richly colored work also seems to pay homage to Matisse, and, even to the untrained eye, is delightful to look at. His colors seem to generate a light of their own, lending even a windowless gallery a sense of being sun-swept.

"Picasso has said that painting is love made visible, and that occurs to me whenever I create something," De Niro once said. "If you can't express love, what's the use of expressing anything?"

A conversation with Robert De Niro, Sr., is a conversation with a wise and soft-spoken man who seems at ease and pleased with the choices he has made in his illustrious life. He stands a couple of inches shy of six feet. His squarish head with its sharp features is topped with a mass of dark and gray locks—suggesting at once an impression of Beethoven. On their way to forming a smile, his lips definitely suggest Robert De Niro, the actor. He dresses casually—a flannel shirt, corduroys, sneakers. When he speaks, he is very solicitous of his listeners and ever ready to engage them in a range of topics from machismo in Abstract Expressionist art, to Hemingway, Rimbaud, the Paris he remembers and plans to go back to, to a recent trip to Atlantic City with Virginia Admiral to hear Diahnne Abbott (his daughter-in-law) sing, to the current "impersonal" trends in Abstract art. The listeners feel they are being treated, royally, to glimpses of the artist's life. Robert De Niro, Sr., radiates warmth, curiosity, and empathy. His handshake alone is worth a thousand words.

Berta Walker, director of New York's Graham Gallery, speaks of the artist's enduring achievements. "Robert De Niro has been an established artist for more than thirty-five years, exhibiting with the American Abstract Expressionists at the Peggy Guggenheim Gallery as early as 1947. Through hard work and dedication he has developed complete control over the light, color, and line that inhabit his landscapes and still lifes. This ability to incorporate the skill and knowledge of his art, with the clarity of his vision, is the basis for his accomplishments as a painter—the result being a labor of love, an expression of his experience. Today, he is truly an American master."

"I also think that painting must be fun," says De Niro. "Mondrian said he would rather stop painting than paint what other people want from him." De Niro's love of painting, his single-minded commitment to his craft, seems to have emerged when he was five years old. "Why? I don't know—I was very isolated." Robert De Niro, the actor, a man with very similar drives indeed, wanted to act from the age of ten. "It seemed he always wanted to be an actor," the father has recalled, "although he tried both art and music for a short time."

Robert and Virginia De Niro separated when their only child was two. Painting and sculpting were a matter of life and death to the artists, and both parents— who have remained friends over the years following their divorce—fought very hard to create their own artistic destiny. A friend of the family has said, "Like so many children of that powerful postwar generation of

New York artists, the young De Niro wasn't coddled by his parents. . . . Bobby was out in the streets a lot as a child. He wasn't being rebellious. That's just the way the cookie crumbled."

A Fashionable Watering Place, a collection of poems privately published by Robert De Niro, Sr., in 1976, represents a written portrait of the artist. It is an alternately sentimental and tough volume comprised of sixty-seven poems, written during and about his years at home and abroad, from 1941 to 1976. In it, he pays homage to places—New York, Africa, Spain, Calcutta, France—and figures who have influenced his life and his art. The volume contains twelve poems that honor Greta Garbo in *Camille,* and others that invoke such figures as Rimbaud, Lautreamont, Gide, and Gertrude Stein. The volume is abundant with images of French cafés, exotic blackamoor dancers, roses, and those whom the artist has loved. It offers a lingering taste of what it was like to be a struggling, widely travelled artist with an abundance of ambition, imagination, spirit, and, occasionally, a scarcity of funds. *A Fashionable Watering Place* is a compelling testament to the bittersweet years of an artist's struggle for recognition. With a curious mixture of pride and characteristic De Niro self-assertion, this inscription appears following the table of contents: "These poems are by Robert De Niro the Painter, not to be confused with Robert De Niro the actor, his son." Has his son's illustrious film career had a helpful or hindering effect on his own work and career? "It creates a certain interest. But it can overshadow you. Anyway, the people he and I relate to are in two different worlds."

As a child, Robert De Niro, the actor, was extremely shy, a character trait that, to this day, beguiles and often frustrates even the most intrepid of interviewers and sends them scurrying off to friends and colleagues of the actor, in hopes of fleshing out copy in time for tomorrow's deadline. At the age of ten, in Manhattan's P.S. 41, Robert played the role of the Cowardly Lion in *The Wizard of Oz*. Already, it appeared, the young De Niro was able to express himself when playacting. By the time he was sixteen, the streets of Little Italy presented a more compelling brand of education than did school. "I had a bad high school scene," he has said. "I was at Rhodes. I went to Music and Art. One semester. It was a good school. I should have stayed there." Once his mother said, "His idea of high school was just not to show up."

At sixteen, he earned his first paycheck as a working actor, on a tour of high schools in the metropolitan area, in Chekhov's *The Bear*. Clearly, by this time, Robert De Niro was his own man, about to embark on a fifteen-year journey of nights on the stages of countless workshop theaters, college tours, and even the dinner theater circuits in metropolitan suburbia. He appeared in such standard fare as *Cyrano de Bergerac, Compulsion, Long Day's Journey into Night, Generation,* and *Tchin-Tchin.*

His Off-Broadway forays included Jackie Curtis' *Glamour, Glory and Gold,* Shelley Winters' *One Night Stands of a Noisy Passenger,* Merle Molofsky's *Kool-Aid,* presented by the Repertory Theater of Lincoln Center, and Julie Bovasso's *Schubert's Last Serenade.* During this time he was able to study under such drama teachers as Stella Adler, Luther James, and Lee Strasberg. Once, in those early days, he was asked by a director why he wanted to be an actor. "I told him I didn't know," De Niro said. "He said, 'You want to be an actor to express yourself.' And later on, when I got into acting seriously, I remembered this and I said that *is* the reason I want to be an actor—to express myself."

II

The Method to His Madness

Stella Adler, the chief American exponent of the Stanislavski method of acting, implores her students to employ "your creative imagination," to create a past that belongs to the character. "Your life is one-millionth of what you know. Your talent is in your imagination: the rest is lice." She urges students to employ props, a sense of art and architecture, and physical action as they become their character. "Acting is action, action is doing. Find ways to do it, not to say it." At the Stella Adler Conservatory, a typical course in Advanced Character may employ the use of photographic slides to press upon students some of the broader tenets of Adler's method: as a slide of waves breaking on a coastline appears, Adler speaks to her students of life's primary struggles—the force of good versus evil, God versus Satan, and so on. She speaks of man's need to achieve, to rise, and to conquer nature rather than be pulled down by it. "I want you to get that force in you," she tells her class. On the screen, images of mountains or of trees bending in the wind or bearing a winter snow on their branches all drive the point home to students: acquire the power of stone; endure galelike adversity with inner resilience; learn to bear up under the pressure of a winter of burdens. "You have to know how man emerged," she says, "how he built edifices and churches, how he surrounded himself with an army. It all has to be built from the beginning, so the actor is completely controlled by the culture of the period. If you don't know Versailles and you don't know the king, then you don't know what power is." Heady, invigorating stuff from a lady who has commanded the respect and awe of more than one generation of American actors. She "curses, cajoles, rages, roars, and from time to time even compliments her students," said *The New York Times.* Of the art of teaching actors, the art at which she stands at the apex, she says, "The teacher has to inspire. The teacher has to agitate. You cannot teach acting. You can only stimulate what's already there."

One former Adler student, currently an actor, playwright, and co-founder of Manhattan Class Company, a New York-based theater development and production company, recalls how as a student enrolled in New York University's B.F.A. program, he and others were "farmed out" to the Adler Conservatory, which, along with the Strasberg Institute and the Circle-in-the-Square, is an adjunct to N.Y.U.'s training program in acting. "On our first day," he recalls, "we met Adler's assistant, who was to run the class. He issued dress code regulations to us: white shirts, pleated and pressed pants, and black shoes for the boys; for the girls, skirts, high-necked blouses, heels, and, of course, hair pinned up off their faces. I felt like I was back in parochial school." It was a tense atmosphere, he recalls. "You had to be good, or forget it. There was no room for making mistakes. Anyway, after three days we met Stella Adler. While she stood listening outside the door, we were taught what to do—practicing over and over again how to rise upon her entrance, while chanting in unison, "Good morning, Miss Adler. We are pleased to meet you and look forward to embarking with you on our journey to discover our art." The atmosphere was charged. "The whole thing was staged as if we were awaiting the arrival of the president. Her assistants were like Secret Service men scouting the area for would-be crackpots or assassins. At any moment I expected to see them talking into their watches." Adler entered. "She was dressed in black and she wore ballet make-up. She accepted our humble supplication and ascended onto the first platform, which created a kind of stage in the classroom, and then onto a second, higher platform to the right of the 'stage,' where she proceeded to seat herself (with the aid of two assistants) upon a red leather arm chair that more than resembled a throne. The whole scene was very intimidating.

"At any rate, one by one, we began performing the simple exercises that had been assigned the day before, while her assistant critiqued them. No sooner would he get ten words out of his mouth when Adler would interrupt him, 'No, Ron, that's wrong,' and would then proceed to contradict everything he had said. Such was the manner in which the class was run. For two days we would have the assistant telling us how to shape our craft, and then Stella Adler would come in and contradict it all. She was an outrageous personality. Sometimes derogatory, often heartless, but always fascinating to watch. But at nineteen, I didn't want to be told what was right and what was wrong in acting. I wanted the freedom to explore my own process. I needed to be able to make mistakes . . . so I got out."

If Stella Adler has taught acting with an emphasis on external stimulation—creating a character from the outside in—Lee Strasberg, the other major exponent of Stanislavski's method of acting, sought to instill actors with a sense of the importance of drawing from within themselves first to find a character—creating from the inside out. At his Actors Studio, a sort of gymnasium for professional actors, he drove followers further and further into their memories until they found a personal experience to form their character. Affective memory, the most well-known tenet of the Strasberg technique, involves an actor's choosing a personal experience that is parallel to a particular moment in a scene. In his book, *A Method to Their Madness,* Foster Hirsch quotes Strasberg: "The key is in the concentration on the object. . . . The memory does not fade, take my word for it. . . . Our experiences are literally engraved in the nervous system. They are woven into the fabric of our existence and can be relived, though we usually don't like these things awakened."

Strasberg encouraged actors to "enrich the author's work by writing a subtext triggered by emotional and sensory memories," Hirsch says. "Adler tells students to remain within the place and situation of the play. [Her] idea is that the actor claims personal possession of the playwright's words not through self-analysis, as at the Studio, but by stepping out of himself, allowing his imagination to take flight from clues the author has planted."

From 1973 to 1976, Robert De Niro was an ob
server and occasional guest performer at the Actor:
Studio. On the subject of Method acting he once said
"Of course, you always bring something of yourself to
a part, but to me acting means playing different parts
trying to get as close to the reality of a character as
possible, learning his life-style, how he holds his fork.
how he carries himself, how he talks, how he relates to
other people. It's hard to do, because it means you
always have to keep looking. Some days you find nothing, other days you're inspired and you see lots that's
exciting. That's why I like to travel before I do a part
. . . so I can feel I've prepared as well as I can. I want
to feel I've earned the right to play a person."

Robert De Niro stands at the crossroads of the
Adler and Strasberg techniques (both rooted in the Stan-
islavskian notion of literally becoming a character). He
has said, "At first being a star was a big part of it. When
I got into it, it became more complicated. To totally
submerge into another character and experience life
through him, without having to risk the real-life conse-
quences—well, it's a cheap way to do things you would
never dare to do yourself." In 1960, De Niro began to
take acting seriously enough to enroll in various acting
classes, chiefly in Stella Adler's. She was the first teacher
who gave him "a total sense of theater and character."
In a recent interview, De Niro says, "I don't want you
to think one method is better that the other. They're
different. Stella Adler's was more straight Stanislavski.
Lee Strasberg at Actors Studio was doing another thing.
I studied with Stella for about three years."

The late sixties saw the Off-Broadway production
of Jackie Curtis' *Glamour, Glory and Gold,* subtitled
"The Life and Legend of Nola Noonan: Goddess and

Star." It was the story of an ambitious Chicago waitress who achieved Hollywood fame only to lose it all to booze. Its first run, in 1968—it was revived in 1974, with the author in the lead—did not open to uniformly good reviews. One critic wrote that "the author and director make a fatal mistake in not demonstrating any point of view about the material." That critic, writing in the *Village Voice*, was impressed however by a young newcomer to the stage. Robert De Niro, in his variety of roles as Nola's boyfriends and leading men, ". . . made clean, distinct character statements in a series of parts which many actors would have fused into a general mush. De Niro is new on the scene and deserves to be welcomed."

Sally Kirkland, who later appeared with De Niro in Shelley Winters' *One Night Stands of a Noisy Passenger,* recalled seeing De Niro in *Glamour, Glory and Gold:* "He played five parts. I'd never seen anything so brilliant. I went backstage and told him, 'Do you know that you are going to be the most incredible star?' He was unbelievably shy. I thought perhaps I was embarrassing him. But I could tell that more than anything, he wanted to believe it."

Robert De Niro's first film break came in 1968, with the release of Brian De Palma's *Greetings,* probably the first successful "youth" film of the sixties (it prefigured *Easy Rider*). De Palma has said, "It dealt with more than getting stoned and chasing girls. It said that kids cared about Vietnam, the draft, assassinations, and the politics of sex." De Niro played the role of Jon Rubin, a porno filmmaker, voyeur and one of three men trying to evade the draft. Starring with him were Jonathan Warden and Gerritt Graham. They formed a sort of counterculture triad, romping around the New

York metropolitan area (à la the Beatles in Richard Lester's *A Hard Day's Night*), devising ways to flunk their induction physicals. The film was aimed at the growing youth market and sought to exploit the accelerating anti-Vietnam war sentiment in the United States. Its opening sequence, in fact, showed President Lyndon B. Johnson on television, trying to drum up support for the war: "I'm not saying you never had it so good," he says, "but that's true, isn't it?"

Computer dating and voyeurism were among *Greetings'* preoccupations, yet it has been said that if anything saved the film from being merely a jokey, subculture collage, it was what critic Michael Bliss has called its "subtext of violence" and its depiction of a time of ruptured idealism and disenchantment in America following the assassination of John F. Kennedy. *Greetings* won Berlin's Silver Bear Award, and its sequel, *Hi, Mom!*, would again see Robert De Niro as Jon Rubin, the cinematic precursor to his much later screen creation, Travis Bickle.

In an effort to exploit the unexpected vogue for *Greetings*, Brian De Palma released *The Wedding Party* in 1969. It had been sitting on the shelf for six years. One of the director's earliest films, it was made while he was studying for a graduate degree at Sarah Lawrence College, in Bronxville, New York. De Palma recalls the young Robert De Niro's audition. "He was very mild, shy, self-effacing. . . . Nobody knew him. He was only a kid of nineteen. He read for the movie and then asked to do an improvisation from *Waiting for Lefty*. He went out and then came back in like a powerhouse. He came on like Broderick Crawford—reading a speech to the cabbies in the union hall. He was simply great—that I remember." *The Wedding Party* captured Robert De Niro on film for the first time. "He got fifty dollars for the whole thing," says De Palma.

Like *Greetings,* and many films that would follow in De Niro's illustrious career, *The Wedding Party* focused on male camaraderie. Its subjects were three pals, one of them fast approaching his wedding day, while the other two (with De Niro as Cecil) try to convince him to escape. The action took place on a palatial estate among the family members of the bride-to-be (Jill Clayburgh). The film employed the then-unconventional techniques of quick-cut editing combined with fast-locomotion—lending a jerky, funny, Keystone Kops effect to the action. In this uneven satire of traditional values, confusion, and tension attendant upon the nuptial day, De Niro played his role like a third stooge, or a Ringo Starr. And his appearance was very strange: with his crew-cut hairstyle and his extra weight he looked portentously like a younger, smaller version of the inflated Jake La Motta in *Raging Bull*—the stunning portrayal that, eleven years later, would win him an Academy Award.

The Wedding Party opened to generally supportive reviews and was perceived by one critic as a "delightful film" that "keeps the normal desire of young lovers within the bounds of decency." This was undoubtedly a twist in 1969, when the Beatles were singing "Why Don't We Do It in the Road," and Broadway was bouncing to the undulating in-the-buff rhythms of *Oh! Calcutta!* and *Hair!*

With the De Palma films under his belt, Robert De Niro was chosen by Roger Corman (at the suggestion of Shelley Winters) to play the role of Lloyd Barker, the ill-fated junkie son of Kate ("Ma") Barker in *Bloody Mama,* with Shelley Winters in the lead. *Bloody Mama* was a fast-paced, sizzling crime melodrama based upon the lives of the infamous Barker clan, who terrorized Arkansas during the Depression. In 1936, F.B.I. director J. Edgar Hoover called Ma Barker ". . . the most vicious, dangerous, and resourceful criminal brain this country has produced in years. . . . Mother Barker brought about bank robberies, hold-ups, a kidnapping and commanded the slaying of some who only a short time before enjoyed what they thought was her friendship. Yet, she liked to hum hymns and at one time of her life, at least, she was deeply religious and a regular church attendant."

Bloody Mama, shot in five-and-a-half weeks and released when Robert Kennedy's assassination was still fresh in the minds of Americans, garnered a wide variety of critical responses. Its decidedly unromantic, unsentimental portrayal of Ma Barker and her incestuous crew of dim-witted animal-boys was in sharp contrast to the more whitewashed, sentimental treatment of *Bonnie and Clyde,* which was showing in cinemas at the time.

As Lloyd Barker, Ma Barker's youngest son, Robert De Niro portrayed perfectly a fractured, disconnected, drug-crazed person. Though his scenes were relatively brief, they were imbued with his character's spiritual bankruptcy, with a schizoid, paranoid intensity. It was a stunningly disturbing portrayal, and one that more than raised eyebrows on the set.

"I tell you," Shelley Winters says, "Bobby gets to the kernel, the soul of a character, and he refuses to let go. . . . The character he was playing in *Bloody Mama* was supposed to deteriorate physically, and Bobby got so frail that we all became alarmed. His face got this horrible chalky look and his skin broke out in disgusting sores. At night, we'd all go out to dinner and stuff our-

selves and there Bobby would sit, drinking *water*. I
don't think he ate a bite of food during the entire shooting of the movie. He must have lost at least thirty
pounds."

Remembering one of the lighter moments during
the shooting of the film, Miss Winters said, "This is
going to sound crazy, but . . . Bobby got killed in *Bloody
Mama*. His part was over and he could have gone
home. On the day we were to shoot the burial scene,
I walked over to the grave, looked down and got the
shock of my life. 'Bobby!' I screamed, 'I don't believe
this! You come out of that grave this minute!' "

The first time she ever saw Robert De Niro perform, Miss Winters says, was ". . . in some loft in the
Village—an experimental play. When he moved across
the stage it was like lightning. Gave me tingles. I hadn't
felt or seen anything like that since the forties, when I
saw Brando in a four-performance flop."

Yet, in public, Miss Winters says, "he almost never
shows emotion. . . . But once . . . in New York, I gave
a Thanksgiving party. Invited all my theatrical waifs,
my babies. Bobby was there, waiting for his date, a
young actress he had a crush on. She didn't show up
until dessert. She sort of floated in. 'Oh, hi, Bobby . . .' He went into the bedroom and pounded the
headboard with his fist. He never talked to her again."

III

Successful
Hippie

In 1970, Robert De Niro was again featured in a Brian De Palma contemporary social satire. *Hi, Mom!* was a sequel to *Greetings*, chronicling the continuing urban adventures of the Vietnam vet, Jon Rubin.

In this spoof of white liberals, black militants, voyeuristic filmmakers, and urban guerrillas, De Niro's Rubin sets up house in a seedy apartment building for the purpose of filming the sexual activities of his neighbors. He becomes the protégé of a pudgy master pornographer (Allen Garfield), and both of them manage to fail in all of their cinematic escapades. From this point on, what *Time* called the film's "conglomeration of wild humor, fantasy and racial issue" moves into a compelling, forceful play-within-the-film called *Be Black, Baby.* In the "play," the audience is forced into what Michael Bliss has called "confrontational situations with members of the troupe. The actors in the troupe have painted their faces white; the audience's faces are painted black, and the two groups exchange roles." At first, the traditional barrier between audience and actors is politely maintained. But finally, as the "white" actors become increasingly abusive to the "black" audience members, a major disruption ensues. In this brilliant sequence, Bliss says, "not only are the barriers between the audience (theater *and* film audience) and actors broken down, but we completely forget the contrived nature of *Hi, Mom!*'s preceding action."

Enter Robert De Niro, this time as an angry club-swinging policeman. He pushes, he shoves members of the audience up against walls, calls them "niggers," and reveals early in his career what Bliss calls "a terrifying capacity . . . for the depiction of violence-prone individuals." Bliss maintains that many of De Niro's "mature acting gestures" were already in evidence in *Greetings* and that in *Hi, Mom!* a prototype of *Taxi Driver*'s Travis Bickle was in full swing: "In De Niro's challenging yell to one of the whites ('What did you say? What are you gonna do about it?') we can hear a frightening anticipation of Travis' 'You talkin' to me?'" There is also a scene in *Hi, Mom!* where De Niro tips over a television set and then shoots it. "An awesomely accurate precursor," Bliss says, "of the *Taxi Driver* scene in which Travis tips over his television while fondling one of the deadly weapons he purchased from gun salesman Andy."

One curious note of criticism in response to *Hi, Mom!* came from *The New Republic*. "De Niro . . . was very good as part of a troika in the first picture but lacks the range and appeal to sustain a film more or less by himself." History would write a much different review.

One Night Stands of a Noisy Passenger, written by Shelley Winters and produced at Actors Playhouse in December 1970, did not open to generous reviews. The work comprised three one-act plays, the third of which starred Diane Ladd and Robert De Niro as an unlikely pair of bedmates: she as an over-the-hill Oscar-winning actress who made a wrong turn somewhere in Laurel Canyon, and he, as the karate-chopping, bisexual Method-acting hippie in whose bed she crash-lands after dropping a tab of acid.

Any interest generated by Miss Winters' admission of autobiographical material in the play did not help sustain the show's run. Nor, of course, did an Off-Broadway theater strike in the early part of December 1970. *One Night Stands of a Noisy Passenger* closed after seven performances.

The show chronicled three phases of an Academy Award–winning actress' life. Its first segment, called "The Noisy Passenger" (starring Richard Lynch and Sally Kirkland), concerned the political awakening of a budding actress and her relationship with her Marxist mentor. "Une Passage" (starring Sam Schacht and Elizabeth Franz) saw that actress in a hotel room in Rome a few years later, with another mentor-lover, this time a married Hollywood producer. "Last Stand" was the third segment, starring Robert De Niro and Diane Ladd. De Niro's role presented him in a caustic, truculent style that he would hone in the years to come. The running dialogue between the two characters took advantage of every pop culture maxim in service at the time, as well as various four-letter words.

Among the play's preoccupations were sex, astrology, fear of aging, and a jaundiced view of show business. A hodgepodge of "enlightened" counter-culture commentary, one of its more sincere moments occurs when the Woman character in one of many non-sequiturs realizes that in life "the fulfillment is not in the end—it is in the act."

De Niro was recommended to Shelley Winters for the part by actress Sylvia Miles. For a fifteen-minute segment in the play that required him to karate-chop a board into two pieces, he studied karate for several months. His performance as the neo-mystical actor-stud generated much excitement. Adjectives like "brilliant," "excellent," and "stunning" were common, and one television commentator excitedly announced that the young De Niro was "an actor to keep your eyes on." *New York*, however, had no kind words for the whole venture, which it felt exuded "a certain fetid, intramural smugness, as of an Actor's Studio exercise, which is really what it is."

A former colleague from the set of *One Night Stands of a Noisy Passenger* recalls sharing a dressing room with De Niro. "He was always very concentrated and, I remember, not given to small talk. He was, even then, a very private person. . . . I always admired his acting enormously. He was terrific onstage, but very quiet backstage. . . . You know, for a time we once shared the same agent for commercials. I can remember sitting next to him one day in an office and our showing our photos to each other. Most actors, you know, have 8 × 10 head shots, but De Niro had what is called a composite photo: a photo that showed four smaller shots with the actor in make-up, as different characters. It wasn't usual for young actors to have composites done. Composites are usually what character actors have made up. But he was character acting, even then."

Playwright Marvin Bevans recalls a Christmas Eve dinner, in 1971, shared with "Bobby" De Niro, Shelley Winters, and Diane Ladd. Offstage, he found the caustic actor-stud De Niro to be "very quiet and unassuming. He was totally relaxed, unpretentious and attractive in a shy, vulnerable way. He had just seen *The Gang That Couldn't Shoot Straight,* in which De Niro played; he seemed embarrassed by it . . . he had a nice aura—you knew he would be famous one day. I remember he was very friendly with Shelley."

Shelley Winters was linked romantically to Robert De Niro then, and she has since spoken fondly of those days. "Listen, let's put it this way. I had a bigger romance with Bobby than I did with any of my lovers. Better change that to read 'any of my husbands.' No, I guess lover sounds all right. I'm Bobby's Italian mama," she once said. "Well . . . maybe I *am* his Jewish mama, but if I am, he's my Jewish son. Bobby needs somebody to watch over him. He doesn't even wear a coat in the wintertime. Do you know that when we did *Bloody Mama* down in the Ozarks, he had no idea of how much money he was getting? When I found out how little they were paying him, I demanded they give him something for his *expenses,* at least. Bobby was broke but, of course, he will never borrow, so you have to find ways of giving him money without letting him know you're giving it to him."

In late 1971, yet another pop-culture stage production flopped after five performances. It was called *Kool-Aid,* written by Merle Molofsky, and presented by The Repertory Theatre of Lincoln Center. It starred Barbara eda-Young, Kevin O'Connor, and

Robert De Niro. By this time De Niro had played a variety of character roles Off-Broadway, in regional theaters, on tour, and in film. His role in *Kool-Aid,* which actually comprised two one-act plays—*Three Street Koans* and *Grail Green*—was similar to that which he had perfected in *One Night Stands of a Noisy Passenger.* In *Three Street Koans* he played Fatboy, a hanger-on in a crowd of junkies who inhabit the environs of the Hudson River on Manhattan's Upper West Side. *Three Street Koans* was harsh in its depiction of a junkie mother and her three-year-old addicted daughter, who, after dying of an overdose administered by her mother, is consigned to the cold currents of the Hudson. In *Grail Green,* De Niro played the role of Douglas One, a young denizen of the Age of Aquarius at perpetual odds with his guru, the Counselor. Some of it clever, some of it seeped in cliché, *Kool-Aid* was another swinging commentary that offered drug use and counter-culture hip spiritualism as the antidote to the urban angst and "lousy cardboard lives" endured by the over-thirty generation. Its unevenness certainly reflected the changing times and identity crises that many Americans experienced during the end of the 1960s. And Robert De Niro was there, playing it all out on stage, fast becoming a barometer of those changes.

Julie Bovasso's hilarious cross-cultural farce, *Schubert's Last Serenade,* ran from June 13–17, 1973, at The Manhattan Theatre Club. It was an absurdist romp through the twists and turns of a self-conscious and volatile love affair between Alfred (Robert De Niro), a construction worker, and Bebe (Laura Esterman), a Radcliffe undergraduate. With all of their stage directions sniffily delivered by the maître d' of the exclusive restaurant where they meet for their tryst, Bebe and Alfred rise and plop along the rocky, riotous terrain of an unlikely love. Did Bebe "fall" for Alfred the first time they stumbled across each other in front of the Customs building? And if so, is the bandage around her head a result of that "fall"? Was she falling for Alfred or falling for the "cause"? Would she have fallen for Alfred if she hadn't fallen for the cause? "Is it me or the cause, baby?" Alfred wants to know. Are Alfred and Bebe really in love with each other or in love with being in love? When did Bebe realize that she and Alfred were "on the same side"? Is the union behind it all? Will Franz Schubert continue playing behind the potted palm near the table?

Schubert's Last Serenade raised these and other questions. But there was no question that Robert De Niro, as the gruff, Brandoesque hard-hat Alfred, gave a wonderful, carefully plotted, and broadly humorous performance. Playwright/actress Julie Bovasso recalled De Niro during rehearsals for her play: "For the first week or so of rehearsal I thought, oh my poor play! He arrives at his characterization by what sometimes seems like a very circuitous route. He wanted to do one scene while chewing on breadsticks," she told *Newsweek.* "Dubiously I let him, and for three days I didn't hear a word of my play—it was all garbled up in breadsticks. But I could see something happening, he was making a connection with something, a kind of clown element. At dress rehearsal he showed up without the breadsticks. I said, 'Bobby, where are the breadsticks?' And he said simply, 'I don't need them anymore.' " *Schubert's Last Serenade* was Robert De Niro's last appearance on the stage.

The eagerly anticipated film adaption of Jimmy

Breslin's *The Gang That Couldn't Shoot Straight* opened in December 1971. A long, winding tale of underworld rivalry in Brooklyn, the film was severely criticized. *The New York Times* called it "more of an insult to Mafia efficiency than to small-time Italian criminals in Brooklyn." It was also roundly condemned as an insult to the Italian-American community for all its stereotyped characterizations and for its failure to capture the truly comic sensibilities of Breslin's book. It was a cockeyed comedy rife with heavy-handed religious satire and what was perceived as substandard, unprofessional acting. One critic blasted the film for its actors' "transparently improvised accents." For his role as Mario Trantino, De Niro paid his own way to Italy to learn the Sicilian dialect.

If critics seemed unanimous in their dismissal of the film, they were of one voice in their praise for Robert De Niro. As bicyclist, phony priest, and thieving immigrant from southern Italy, De Niro practically stole the film. He was the only character who came across convincingly. It was De Niro's "impish rogue," one critic wrote, who "provided the proceedings with a vestige of behavioral charm."

De Niro also appeared in a few other films in the early seventies, although from all indications the films were box-office flops. *Born to Win* concerned a junkie hairdresser living in the lower depths of Manhattan. *Jennifer on My Mind* was a black comedy about an aimless, wealthy youth who falls in love with a bored, upper-class suburban girl. In response to her painful pleading, Jennifer's boyfriend fatally injects her with heroin. The film unfolds in flashback, with the opening sequences showing the boyfriend trying to dispose of her body. In *Sam's Song,* De Niro plays a would-be filmmaker working on a documentary about Richard Nixon. In the course of a Long Island weekend, he meets a handful of rich, disenchanted, and alienated characters. As he would say later, "I've been in bad films, but they had good intentions."

IV

Taking Off

By 1972, despite critical commendations, Robert De Niro was not what could be considered a "hot property," but he was being noticed. "I wasn't what you call an attractive person," he has said. "I wasn't snatched up for certain roles in movies. Therefore, I had to work harder . . . the more you become a star the less preparation and hard work seem necessary. There is more temptation not to do right by what you do. But a star really has more responsibility."

Up until this point in his career, 1972, De Niro had garnered much attention for the intensity he brought to a more or less static type of role. Whether as a mild-mannered pornographer-turned-revolutionary *(Greetings, Hi, Mom!)*, a frustrated, angry young man of the counter-culture *(One Night Stands of a Noisy Passenger, Kool-Aid)*, a gruff, absurdist lover *(Schubert's Last Serenade)*, or a drug-abuser and petty-thief *(Bloody*

Mama, The Gang That Couldn't Shoot Straight), De Niro seemed to have cornered the market on alienation, misdemeanor, and arrogance. His roles were brilliantly conceived and economically dispatched. He wasted no gestures. He was already highly respected for all the work he put into a role and was widely perceived as an "actors' actor."

There is a special poignancy about the death of a young athlete. A. E. Housman captured it well when he wrote "To an Athlete Dying Young," with the lines "Smart lad, to slip betimes away/From fields where glory does not stay/And early though the laurel grows/It withers quicker than the rose."

Robert De Niro was chosen for the role of Bruce Pearson, the baseball player with a terminal illness, in the 1973 film *Bang the Drum Slowly.* That year, Robert De Niro's career would take off. The film, based on the 1956 novel by Mark Harris, offered a turning point role for De Niro: that of an essentially sympathetic character, a baseball catcher dying of Hodgkin's disease. The friendship between the dying catcher and his roommate Henry Wiggin (Michael Moriarty) is tenderly explored. Their friendship is sometimes subtle, sometimes overtly chummy, and, more often than not, difficult. *Bang the Drum Slowly* was lauded for the evenhanded way in which it dealt with the dynamics of male camaraderie in an enormously complicated relationship.

"You're driving along with a man who's been told he's dying—it was bad enough rooming with him when he was well." Such are the words of Henry Wiggin, ace pitcher, baseball star, and the only real friend Bruce Pearson ever had. De Niro's Bruce Pearson—not too bright, not very endearing, yet somehow sympathetic—is more than a victim of the disease that will claim his life. He is also victim of a healthy amount of team scorn because of his backwoods ways, his oafishness ("I got to develop brains"), the way he talks, and the way he chews tobacco. All in all, he is not a very popular player, and not even that good a catcher. And no one can understand why Henry Wiggin, who is about to be drafted to another team, is holding out, and will take even less money than his original hold-out figure, on the condition that wherever he goes, Bruce Pearson goes too. Or that if he stays with the Mammoths team Bruce will stay, too—for what will probably be the last season of his life. Soon, with the truth about Pearson's illness in the open, his teammates gradually begin to appreciate him. He is suddenly surrounded by friends who are telling him how great he is and who are goading him on to be a great catcher. The team begins to play better. This exercise in hypocrisy, carefully drawn as Pearson gets closer to death, is complete when there is no representative from the team at his funeral, save for his best friend.

Director John Hancock took his cast and crew to Clearwater, Florida, to pick up some baseball pointers for the film. Filmed in the ballparks of New York's Shea and Yankee stadiums, the "New York Mammoths" received valuable assistance from the New York Mets, New York Yankees, Pittsburgh Pirates, Boston Red Sox, Cleveland Indians, and Philadelphia Phillies. "Each rehearsal day started with two hours of playing baseball," Hancock has said, ". . . it made good feelings happen, it helped create the sense of a team."

"Baseball players are like stars," De Niro said in an interview. "It's always 'Later, kid.' Three weeks before we began shooting I played ball in Central Park . . . it was really hard for me because I never played baseball. I read a book by Del Bethel—he was the coach at CCNY —and he helped me out a lot. And I watched TV and took notes, everything."

De Niro all but lost himself in the role. "I think the way you look has a lot to do with the way you act. That's why I start with a character's looks. When I got the part of Bruce, I learned he was from a small town in Georgia. So I went to Georgia and stayed in a small town. I found an old-fashioned country store. There I bought the kind of clothes Bruce would buy. I wore them all around. Then I worked on the way Bruce would talk. The people in the town were really nice. They didn't mind my copying the way they talk. In fact, they would correct me when I sounded too much like a New Yorker. After awhile, I began to move like Bruce. I began to feel like him, then came the hardest part. I had to learn to chew tobacco. . . ."

"He worked like a dog," John Hancock has said. "He got sick chewing that tobacco, but kept it up until he finally could do it."

"It was a bad experience . . . somebody told me to mix the tobacco with bubble gum. Then I got sticky *and* sick. Finally a local doctor told me that chewing tobacco would make my teeth white. That gave me the courage to keep chewing. I got so I could *look* like I enjoyed it. But it didn't do a thing for my teeth."

For a scene of illness in *Bang the Drum Slowly,* De Niro spun himself around until he got green in the face. "It made me dizzy," he has recalled, "a very similar thing that the character was feeling. I did it so that when we did the take I would feel the character's nauseousness and not have to fake it."

De Niro's Bruce Pearson, thick-headed and seemingly oblivious to everything, including his own impending death, seemed to be saved by his own obtuseness. In one touching sequence in the film, he is hunched over a fire, burning his few possessions, as though to ensure that he would leave no trace of himself behind. "I didn't try to play dumb," De Niro has said, "I just tried to play each scene for where it was. Some people are dumb, but they're not dumb—I guess they're insensitive, but they're not insensitive to everything . . ."

"He reminds me of Alec Guinness, submerging himself completely in his role," Hancock says. "He didn't even want to take off his baseball uniform. He lived in it. Guinness isn't a personality actor; he's a character actor who is also a star—and that's Bobby. But he has an eroticism Guinness never had."

Robert De Niro's "doomed bumpkin," one critic wrote, "is wonderfully exasperating, one of the most unsympathetic characters ever to win an audience's sympathy." Sentimental without being maudlin, *Bang the Drum Slowly* was saluted by critics and filmgoers alike for its warmth and gentle humor. It was the kind of film that, like *Brian's Song,* left the viewer sensitized —and increasingly aware that De Niro, through a magical performance and tender rendering of a born loser doubly condemned, was destined for stardom. His hard-hitting, poignant portrayal of Bruce Pearson won him the 1973 New York Film Critics Award.

On the heels of *Bang the Drum Slowly* came Martin Scorsese's *Mean Streets,* also in 1973. The furor it created is by now legendary, as are the excellent reviews De Niro captured as Johnny Boy, the movie's ill-fated, crazy, aspiring Mafioso hoodlum.

With *Mean Streets,* the first De Niro/Scorsese col-

laboration, the pair made the film community sit up—
or, rather, jump up—and take notice. A graduate of
New York University, Scorsese had a number of films
under his belt: *What's a Nice Girl Like You Doing in
a Place Like This?* (1963), *It's Not Just You, Murray!*
(1964), *The Big Shave* (1967), *Who's That Knocking at
My Door?* (1969), *Street Scenes 1970* (1970), *Medicine
Ball Caravan* (1971), *Elvis on Tour* (1972), and *Box Car
Bertha* (1972). The last was made under the auspices of
Roger Corman. "The most important thing about *Boxcar* was . . . that without making *Boxcar* we could not
have made *Mean Streets,*" Scorsese has said, "because
we used practically the same crew, the same people,
like a Roger Corman production. In other words, it
taught me how to make a film."

Doing a film like *Mean Streets* was, in a way, like
doing a home movie. In fact, more than a handful of
Scorsese's films were shot in Little Italy, where he, like
Robert De Niro, grew up. "We'd never worked together, I'd never seen any of his work—I'd heard about
him, of course," Scorsese has said. "The funny thing was
we met at somebody's house for dinner and I said, 'I
know you.' 'I don't know you,' he said. 'Didn't you used
to hang around Hester Street? Kenmare Street?' It was
he. We hadn't seen each other in fourteen years. . . . I
had never seen Bobby act when I cast him in *Mean
Streets*. We just talked. He was wearing a hat, tilted it
a certain way, saying he thought the character would
wear it that way, and I hired him. Bobby has great
instincts. I trust his choices . . . [he] was perfect for the
part because he knows the life. *Mean Streets* is all about
that, and that's what Bob used to do—hang around
. . . he was a shy kid, a very nice kid, and never one to
make trouble." Scorsese has also said, "We see things

the same way. We both have the sense of being outsiders."

"In Martin," Scorsese's ex-wife Julia Cameron once said, "Bobby has found the one person who will talk for fifteen minutes on how a character would tie a knot. I've seen them go for ten hours nonstop."

Mean Streets examines small-time corruption and thievery in Little Italy. A film about crime operation in a second- and third-generation religious Sicilian family, it is also a study of friendship, power, guilt, and redemption. "You don't make up for your sins in church," Charlie (Harvey Keitel) says as *Mean Streets* begins. "You make up for them in the streets or home." Charlie is a young hood trying hard, very hard, to climb up the ladder from small-time crook to a position of power and respect among his sub-Mafioso pals. His aspirations to be the big fish in Little Italy's small pond are hampered by a few things: his Catholic guilt, his troublesome friend Johnny Boy (De Niro), and his girlfriend Teresa (Amy Robinson), an epileptic, from whom his uncle has warned him to stay away. Without the good blessings of his uncle—who *is* a big fish in the small pond—Charlie has little chance of succeeding, as the manager of a restaurant being extorted by his uncle. His uncle has also told Charlie that he should stay away from Johnny Boy, whose debts are giving Charlie, his only friend, a bad name.

Johnny Boy is a wild, errant punk. A hot-headed person with loyalties to no one, he gets his kicks starting barroom brawls, or by blowing up mailboxes, and by not paying his debts. He has no job, can never hold onto one, and when Michael (Richard Romans), his chief lender, cannot find him, he pressures Charlie.

De Niro's Johnny Boy virtually flows out of the

actor. It is a riveting, shocking performance, incorporating so much of Hester and Kenmare streets that one critic was prompted to say about De Niro, "You'd swear he's been on the street, in the gutter, all his life." Redeeming his every fraud and deception with a toothy grin or a swat, Johnny Boy, more than anyone else in *Mean Streets*—more than Charlie, to be sure—is his own man. He is owned by no one, directed by no one, save his own white flash of chaotic energy. He's the kind of guy who, just for the hell of it, will climb up to a roof top and fire bullets into empty apartments. His schizoid antics prove to be his undoing—and Charlie's, too.

In the film's rain-slicked finale, Johnny Boy has used up the last of Michael's ebbing good graces and has made a fool of him for all to see. In an effort to lie low for awhile, Charlie—the bearer of all of Johnny Boy's sins—takes his friend, and Teresa, away from Little Italy to escape Michael's certain retribution. They drive toward Brooklyn, but soon Michael pulls up alongside their car. After crossing the Brooklyn Bridge, their ride comes to its end, as Michael's companion (Martin Scorsese) fires at Johnny Boy and Charlie. *Mean Streets* ends with vengeance fulfilled.

Mean Streets, an entry in the 1973 New York Film Festival, was widely praised for the realism its players evinced—about one-third of the script was improvised—and for Scorsese's raw footage shot with a hand-held camera. Writing in *Newsweek,* Paul Zimmerman lauded Martin Scorsese for his "jagged editing, his lurid palette of plush reds and blues," and "his rasping rock 'n' roll soundtrack spiced with Italian favorites," all expressing perfectly "the restless violent lifestyle" of the film's young protagonists.

Of Robert De Niro's portrayal of Johnny Boy, *Newsweek* said that "De Niro's vivid performance should be preserved in a time capsule." Film critic Pauline Kael, writing of his uncanny ability to move beyond merely hitting a "true note" to hitting "the far-out, flamboyant one" to "make his own truth," said: "He's a bravura actor, and those who registered him only as the grinning, tobacco-chewing dolt of . . . *Bang the Drum Slowly* will be unprepared for his volatile performance."

It was *Bang the Drum Slowly* and *Mean Streets* that saw a shift in Robert De Niro's career. Henceforth, the category of "promising actor"—a category in which he had labored for at least five years—would be a thing of the past. His role as Johnny Boy was singled out by *Time* as "beautifully realized," and he was voted best supporting actor by the National Society of Film Critics and the New York Film Critics Circle.

One note of dissent among the chords of praise accorded De Niro for his flashy performance came from writer Foster Hirsch. "De Niro is a virtuoso actor, but as Johnny Boy he's not an original: the territory has already been staked-out classically by Marlon Brando in *On the Waterfront.*" The Brando connection to De Niro's Johnny Boy was perceived by more than one person. In fact, it was after seeing *Mean Streets* that a young director, whose film *The Godfather* had made box-office history, also took note: Francis Ford Coppola was convinced that De Niro would do fine, just fine, as the young Don Corleone in *The Godfather, Part II*, the role originated by Marlon Brando in *The Godfather.*

V

Approximately Brando

Francis Ford Coppola's first sweeping epic depicted the blood battles and gang wars of a handful of powerful Mafia "families," played out on the streets of New York. *The Godfather* presented filmgoers with a vivid history lesson of the fictional Corleone family and their reign over organized crime in America. The film put actors like Robert Duvall, Al Pacino, James Caan, and John Cazale on the movie map and marked the return to the screen of one of America's most heralded actors, Marlon Brando, as Mafia chieftain Don Vito Corleone. Robert De Niro was chosen to play the young Corleone in *The Godfather, Part II*.

Marlon Brando's Corleone was the embodiment of power, restrained, kept-in-check, wise power, power that was the result of more than just presiding over the most spectacular Mafia family of post–World War II America. It was money power, an awesome power that was the sum of controlling interests in East Coast and West Coast gambling and the unions, the sum of having cops, judges, politicos, and an assorted gallery of professionals of all kinds deep in his pockets. He had the quiet strength wielded by those with an arsenal of influential friends and subjects. Those who would kiss his ring formed the group to whom favors were granted, and from whom favors were expected in return, at a time of need, in a year, maybe, or perhaps ten. Brando as Corleone evinced the power of love: father to his sons, loving husband, grandfather. He was vested with an awesome respect—and secure, with an octopuslike hold on crime's murky territory, and with a knack for retribution, a knack that would really rather not be tested; an abhorrence of violence, actually. He was a man proud of his achievements: from his long journey as a youngster from Sicily to Ellis Island, America, to his powerful coming-of-age on New York City's Lower East Side.

In *The Godfather, Part II*, Robert De Niro depicted Don Vito Corleone's coming-of-age in an Oscar-winning performance. Every gesture, every nuance that comprised the behavioral traits of Brando's Corleone, De Niro in his role had to "create" and make happen for the first time. He would shape the young Vito's rise up through the ranks of crime in his community, as he protected his people (poor, like himself) and reared his family.

De Niro spent a great deal of time in Sicily in order to prepare for his role as the young Don Corleone. It was there he perfected his Italian—a language he was already familiar with from an earlier visit and from a crash course at Berlitz. He saw *The Godfather* numerous times, paying scrupulous attention to all the gestures and mannerisms that Brando incorporated into his powerful role. "I didn't want to do an imitation," De Niro has said, "but I wanted to make it believable that I could be him as a young man. I would see some little movements that he would do and try to link them with my performance. It was like a mathematical problem— having a result and figuring out how to make the beginning fit." And, he says, "there was a little pressure because I couldn't tell if the choices were good. I made 'em and went with 'em, because you've got to trust the director and trusting Francis Coppola is very easy. There is a thin line between identification and imitation. I wanted to seem like the young guy who ends up the older Godfather. We couldn't look alike because my face is so different than his. [Makeup artist] Dick Smith and I experimented with makeup but it was his idea to go simple and I agreed. I feel it's better to do less than more. What I did was watch videotapes of Brando's scenes, looking for gestures or movements to pick up. Or maybe just a variation on something he did. The voice we tried at first. I was afraid it might be going too far and that it was too raspy. I think it turned out pretty good, though."

De Niro's mathematical efforts certainly paid off handsomely. At the forty-seventh Annual Academy Awards, held on April 8, 1975, *The Godfather, Part II* won six Oscars: for best picture (the contenders were *Chinatown, The Conversation, Lenny,* and *The Towering Inferno*), best director, best supporting actor, best script, best art/set direction, and best original dramatic score. De Niro and costars Michael V. Gazzo and Lee Strasberg were all nominated for best supporting actor, but it was De Niro who won the coveted statuette, thus seeing sixteen years of hard work and devotion to his

craft receive the universal recognition it so rightly de-
served. Ironically, though, De Niro (whose name at this
time was generally preceded in the press with adjectives like "reclusive" and "Garboesque") was not on
hand for this great moment in his career. He was in
Italy with Bernardo Bertolucci, filming the acclaimed
Italian director's turn-of-the-century epic *1900*, a film
that wouldn't be released in the United States for two
more years. His award was accepted by his director,
Francis Ford Coppola. "I'm happy one of my boys
made it . . . he is an extraordinary actor who'll enrich
the film medium for years to come."

"Bobby is a strange, dark figure," Coppola has said.
"I don't know from where he's looking at me. But I'm
comfortable with him. . . . I would not hesitate to cast
Bobby De Niro in any role whatsoever—from a little
street rat to Valentino. I think he's going to be one of
the major stars and give a whole string of incredible
performances. Of course, he likes things I don't like.
The only thing we agree on is that I like him but I'm
not even sure if we agree on that. I like him but I don't
know if he likes himself."

"I have to be able to talk to my director. I must
know what he thinks or we shouldn't be working together." Robert De Niro found in Francis Ford Coppola what he most looked for in a director, sympathy,
and he found a director who respects the actor, who
makes his actors feel comfortable, allowing them to feel
that they are contributing to the work in progress; a
director who allows actors to express their own ideas
and who "like a coach," De Niro says, is supportive.
During the filming of *The Godfather, Part II*, a son of
an artist presented another son of an artist with a token
of gratitude: De Niro gave Coppola a painting by Rob-

ert De Niro, Sr. Carmine Coppola, father of the director, is a composer and conducter and he, along with Nino Rota, received an Oscar for the score of *The Godfather, Part II.*

On the subject of actor and Oscar, De Niro has said, "Lots of people who win the award don't deserve it, so it makes you a little cynical about how much it means. Did it mean that much to me? Well, I don't know. It changes your life like anything that will change your life. People react to it. I mean, it's not bad winning it." De Niro was right to be playing the young Corleone, Brando's role, film critic Pauline Kael wrote, "because he has the physical audacity, the grace, and the instinct to become a great actor—perhaps as great as Brando."

VI

Wanting to Be a Person Like Other People

"On every street in every city in this country there's a nobody who dreams of being somebody. He's a lonely forgotten man desperate to prove that he's alive. . . ."

In 1976, Robert De Niro's Dostoevskian underground man, Travis Bickle, sprung onto the scene—Martin Scorsese's lurid cityscape—like a lethal jack-in-the-box. The vivid, nearly X-rated carnage he unleashed in *Taxi Driver*'s finale evoked a storm of controversy, as did the film's chilly epilogue in which Bickle, a Vietnam vet, was universally lauded for his murderous victory over assorted urban sleaze.

The story of *Taxi Driver*, that is to say, the story of Travis Bickle, had some very real beginnings. It sprang from the vivid experiences of Hollywood scriptwriter Paul Schrader's early days in Los Angeles, at a time when he was particularly down and out, experiencing

43

some real-life failures, both professional and personal. Things had hit rock bottom for him in 1972. He had just written his first screenplay, *Pipeline*, and it was, he says, "a total washout." His marriage had broken up, and he was in debt. He found himself wandering around at night from sheer depression—on the streets, in his car, to porn movie houses—for weeks at a time. "That was when the metaphor hit me for *Taxi Driver*," Schrader recalls, "and I realized that was the metaphor I had been looking for: the man who will take anybody, any place for money; the man who moves through the city like a rat through the river; the man who is constantly surrounded by people, yet has no friends; that was my symbol, my metaphor. The film is about a car as the symbol of urban loneliness, a metal coffin."

Schrader gave the script to his agent and went off on his own for about six months. Some time later, he gave it to director Brian De Palma, who passed it on to producers Michael and Julia Phillips. The Phillipses hawked it around in 1972 but no studio wanted to touch it. The problem, said studio executives, was the subject matter. Violence, depression, and loneliness in New York City were not considered good box office. It was around this time that Schrader and the Phillipses saw a rough cut of *Mean Streets*. Up until this time, "we were talking about doing *Taxi Driver* with Robert Mulligan and Jeff Bridges," Schrader said in a lengthy article in *Film Comment*. "I was fighting that off because it didn't make any sense to me. Yet, it was a deal and God knows I wanted to see the film made. . . . I saw *Mean Streets* and said, 'That's it. De Niro and Scorsese.' They saw it and said, 'That's it,' too. We never entertained any other possibilities. We stuck with it."

De Niro and Scorsese saw the *Taxi Driver* screenplay and loved it. But time passed, and other projects intervened: Michael and Julia Phillips produced *The Sting,* Martin Scorsese directed *Alice Doesn't Live Here Anymore,* and Robert De Niro triumphed in *The Godfather, Part II.* "*Taxi Driver,* whether it lives or dies, is the first film to thoroughly bear the stamp of the new generation in Hollywood and how it operates," Paul Schrader said in 1975. "It was an agreement made three years ago by friends when none of us were bankable. Even after we got successful, we didn't give it up until finally we offered Columbia such a good deal they couldn't turn it down . . . the price tag for the whole creative package—producer, director, star, and screenplay—was $150,000."

Robert De Niro got about $35,000 to do *Taxi Driver* at a time when he was receiving offers for more than ten times that amount. "He was one of the strongest ones behind it all—absolutely adamant about doing it," Schrader says. De Niro felt that *Taxi Driver* was a film people would be watching "fifty years from now, and that whether everybody watched it next year wasn't important." The three of them—De Niro, Scorsese, and Schrader—wanted to do something that would last. They compromised on money, but they didn't compromise on anything else.

So, onto the screen walked Travis Bickle, with a vague resemblance to nearly every misanthrope, mass-murderer, plane-hijacker, or political assassin of the past two decades, and with a vague resemblance, also, to everyman's next-door neighbor. A Vietnam vet with a quirky, lethal charm, he has trouble sleeping at night, so he takes a job as a cabbie, working the graveyard shift, 11:00 P.M. to dawn. De Niro's Travis Bickle longs, as the street's filth unfolds like a nightmare outside his

cab, "to be a person, like other people." It is not easy
to achieve this, with so much of the city's flotsam and
jetsam—whores, hookers, pimps, addicts—encroaching
upon his life. He has no friends, except, perhaps, his
cabbie colleague, the Wizard (Peter Boyle). His attempts to win over Betsy (Cybill Shepherd), a political
campaign worker, fail miserably. Their aborted court-
ship ends at a porn movie theater, the scene of their
first date. "He gravitates toward a violent act," Martin
Scorsese recalls. "The focus of his violence is almost
arbitrarily a political candidate. The movie is about the
forces in his mind that lead him to his destiny . . ."

"It's not the city that's forcing this upon him," Paul
Schrader says, "only his turning up the flame of his own
pressure cooker that drives him increasingly out of
touch with reality."

Rejected by his blonde-haired, blue-eyed Betsy,
Bickle comes upon another female whom he might
save and, in so doing, save himself: Iris (Jodie Foster), a
twelve-year-old prostitute. Bickle wants to rescue her
from the demoralizing life she leads at the hands of her
pimp, Sport (Harvey Keitel). With a failed assassination
attempt on the life of presidential candidate Charles
Palantine (Leonard Harris) already behind him, Bickle
cannot afford to lose in this. His fractured, mohawked
psychosis is already consuming him; and his disgust and
abhorrence of what he sees on the streets, what he
cleans off the back seat of his cab, are surely contributing to his "stomach cancer."

"I was drawn to the script personally because of
the religious aspects," Martin Scorsese says. "There is
an obsessiveness to the character which is very religious
to me. He takes baths. He sips peach brandy. He eats
very odd combinations of food. He keeps a diary, very

ritualistically. His diary is not written the way he speaks. He speaks in a very halting way, but his diary is like poetry. The other thing about this picture which interested me is the idea of sexual repression, and the image of the woman as something she's not—the goddess. The goddess concept is taken from the Virgin Mary. The character is totally obsessed with this blonde-haired, blue-eyed woman, Cybill Shepherd—who is the Virgin Mary—but he could be obsessed with anything at this stage of the game, the way his mind is working. In *Mean Streets,* the guy wants to be recognized for something, but he has nothing tangible to be recognized for. In this case, the cab driver is very similar. He's got something he wants to say but he doesn't know what it is. The character has problems which stem from religion taken to the extreme. I would assume that, at some point in his life, he was very religious." In fact, Scorsese adds, "Travis is a commando for God. And look at the Saints. He's full of their same energy, but his just goes off in a different direction. He sees something ugly or dirty, and he has to clean it up. It's like someone saying, 'You mustn't wear blue, it's against the gods.' He then has to kill you to save your life; in his eyes he's doing good work. Travis has to kill somebody; it doesn't matter whether it's a presidential candidate or a pimp."

Travis Bickle, then, is a cocked gun, an arsenal in deadly waiting. In the film's gruesome finale, Bickle, out to liberate Iris, drives his cab to her apartment. Outside, he fires a shot point-blank at Sport and enters the building where Iris is entertaining a john. And the massacre begins.

"In the scenes of the killing," Scorsese has said, "the slow motion and De Niro's arms . . . we wanted him to look almost like a monster, a robot, King Kong coming to save Fay Wray. Another thing: all of the close-ups of De Niro where he isn't talking were shot forty-eight frames to the second—to draw out and exaggerate his motions. What an actor, to look so great up against a technique like that!"

Taxi Driver's finale, filmed on location in the narrow hallway of an abandoned tenement on Manhattan's Upper West Side, was a special challenge for renowned film makeup artist Dick Smith. His work on *Taxi Driver* involved stabbings, shootings, and mutilations—all shown in graphic terms. He was also hired to do the makeup on De Niro. "De Niro is extremely difficult to work with," said Smith, in an interview with *Cinefantastique*. "He is a paranoid perfectionist. He wants everything he is involved with on a film to be totally real —sets, costumes, makeup, everything—in order to give him a sense his performance is real. . . . I had worked with him previously on *The Godfather, Part II* and I had to put pencil lines on his eyebrows to make his face similar to Brando's. . . . De Niro would scrutinize every single line I drew and criticize them! I deal with something like that as patiently as I can, but when it gets to be too much I say enough!"

Smith achieved the gory effect of a thug having part of his hand blown off by Bickle's .357 Magnum in this way: he made the portion of the hand that remained out of rubber, fitted with tubes to pump blood. This was worn over the actor's real hand. The removable palm and finger section were constructed out of wax. For the shot, the wax portion was blown away by explosive "squibs" placed between it and the rubber appliance, and blood was pumped through.

For his part, Robert De Niro researched his role in

the only way possible—he renewed his taxi license. "I drove with him several nights," Martin Scorsese has said. "He got a strange feeling when he was hacking. He was totally anonymous. People would say anything, do anything in the back seat—it was like he didn't exist. Finally, a guy gets in, a former actor, who recognizes his name on the license. 'Jesus,' he says, 'last year you won the Oscar and now you're driving a cab again.' De Niro said he was only doing research. 'Yeah, Bobby,' says the actor, 'I know. I been there too.'"

De Niro maintained a low profile on the set of *Taxi Driver*. Said one cast member during shooting, "I've been around Bob now for almost three weeks . . . but I can't say I've really exchanged one full sentence with him about anything other than work. In fact, I don't know anymore about him now then I did the first day he walked on the set." Martin Scorsese tries to explain De Niro's reclusiveness while working: "When he works, he just blocks everything and everyone out. . . . Bobby chooses to stay in his trailer and that's it. I knock on his door. I say, 'Can I come in.' He says, 'Sure, sure.' Otherwise I leave him alone."

De Niro wore Paul Schrader's shirt, boots, and belt during the filming of *Taxi Driver*, ("It was spooky to see him in my clothes") and also had Schrader read Arthur Bremer's published diary into a tape recorder. Bremer is the man who shot Alabama governor George Wallace, paralyzing him for life. "I'd want to emphasize that the script was written before any of the diary was published," Schrader says. "After I read the diary, I was very tempted to take some of the good stuff from it and add it to *Taxi Driver*, but I decided not to, because of legal ramifications." Schrader says that the man who brought his Travis Bickle to life "[is] the most exciting, most inventive actor in the country. He teaches you things. He's going to be to a new generation what Brando was. He is amazing and a very introverted man . . ."

A touch of the real was also helpful for De Niro's colleague, Harvey Keitel, who played the pimp Sport: "I met a pimp named Lucky at a bar and we had a good talk. He read the script and made a few suggestions. He told me, for example, 'No, I wouldn't say things like that.' I'm not sure I can reach him because all I have is the phone number of a bar. But I'm wondering if he could be hired as a extra for the scenes I'm in. I think it'd be helpful to have him around . . ."

The entire production of *Taxi Driver* took place in New York City. The interiors were shot in an abandoned Upper West Side brownstone and the film's exteriors were shot in the garment district, the Bellmore Cafeteria on Park Avenue South, around Columbus Circle, and at an Eighth Avenue porno theater. "One day when it was pouring rain, we were filming De Niro in the cab, near Columbus Circle," said Martin Scorsese. "Some businessman in a hurry spotted the cab, came rushing over, and dropped right in. De Niro was so startled all he could do was point to his 'off-duty' sign. The guy bounced right back out, cursing a blue streak all the way down the sidewalk. He never saw the cameras."

Asked during the filming of *Taxi Driver* if he considered himself truly a maker of New York films, Scorsese said, "I don't know. New York is a whole character in *Mean Streets* and *Taxi Driver*, too. I love this city and take it for what it is—it's good and it's bad. I love the fire hydrants squirting water on summer nights and I love the ethnic joking among the crew when we film here. I don't find that in L.A."

Scorsese's formula for working with actors seems to corroborate what De Niro himself looks for in a director. "I find I have to get to know them as human beings first and I really have to like them to be able to coax the best possible performances out of them—and when my actors like me, there's a certain kind of mutual trust that develops. I let them try a lot of things. I let them experiment. But in the back of my mind, I know there are certain things I definitely do not want and other things I do want. By letting them experiment, I usually get what I want sooner or later."

Taxi Driver won the grand prize, the Gold Palm at the Cannes Film Festival in 1976, despite jury chief Tennessee Williams' outburst against violence in films.

In Travis Bickle, a role for which he received an Academy Award nomination in 1976, De Niro brought to the modern screen the alienated, disillusioned psyche of urban anomie—a man seemingly without purpose, without identity, and without any real roots to give his life meaning and continuity. Disconnected from the possibility of authentic relationships with anyone, Travis Bickle's only resort—and it was perhaps a peculiarly American one—was to lash out at everyone around him. Having made his presence felt, he was able to slip back into daily life—ironically, as a hero—and pick up from where he left off. As shocking and farfetched as that all seems, perhaps De Niro and company can be excused for exercising a certain amount of satire or employing poetic license. Nineteen seventy-six, after all, was a time when American values seemed to be turned upside down and when the distinction between right and wrong seemed to be blurred. The controversial war in Vietnam saw the whole concept of "honor" inverted. And in recent political events at least one major indicted co-conspirator in the Watergate scandal had been allowed to go scot-free. As one critic put it in an article about De Niro, it was increasingly difficult to tell the saints from the swine.

"He's a sympathetic figure," insists Scorsese. "There's certainly a lot of Travis in me, some of his same emotions. There are deep, dark things in all of us, and they come out in different ways. I've dealt with mine through analysis; a lot of people release them sexually, but Travis can't even do that."

If *Taxi Driver* and its concerns were a timely essay about violence and disillusion in America, its star became, in the eyes of many, more than just a star. Robert De Niro in 1976 was suddenly a symbol for everyman's quest for identity in a convulsive, uncertain America. He also was said to represent the conflicting, questing energies of his generation, the generation coming to young maturity in the fragmented seventies. All hype, to be sure, but seldom had hype taken on such *meaning*. Suddenly, Robert De Niro personified a sociological dissertation. "At first I was very excited about all the publicity Bobby was getting," said Robert De Niro, Sr., at the time, "but now we're kind of appalled by it."

"I really didn't plan to have so many films in a row with no breaks," Robert De Niro said, alluding to the fact that *1900*, *Taxi Driver*, and *The Last Tycoon* were all filmed back-to-back. "I didn't plan to do that, but I wanted to do this work. In the future, I will keep more time between pictures."

Defense lawyers for would-be presidential assassin, John Hinckley, claimed that he saw *Taxi Driver* at least fifteen times before he shot President Ronald Reagan in 1981. Hinckley's attorneys showed the film at his trial and maintained that he "identified" with Travis Bickle and that he felt that *Taxi Driver* was speaking to him personally. Paul Schrader was more grieved than surprised that *Taxi Driver* might have influenced Hinckley to attempt to take Reagan's life. "It never surprised me that someone could respond so strongly to the story. In most cases it has helped purge people of antisocial behavior. I just regret that it didn't work out that way for Hinckley. But I know what that story means because I know where it came from." Schrader says that the influence *Taxi Driver* had on Hinckley "doesn't mean we should start banning art because if we did, there would be just as many psychopaths. Perhaps more."

Certainly, by 1976, Robert De Niro had what *Newsweek* called "the gestural sophistication of an actor in touch with his primal feelings." One critic said that in all his films De Niro's anger seemed natural and uncontrived: "It is his calm that seems an act." De Niro gave you "the shock of becoming, of a metamorphosis that can be thrilling, moving or frightening." He was motive gone haywire, and his instinctive insight into perverse behavior, his suggestion of positive energy subverted, made him the most expressive actor around. Yet also the most invisible. Actors like Robert Redford, Al Pacino, and Dustin Hoffman cannot go anywhere without causing a scene. But De Niro, on his occasional forays into the public stream, can still slip by unnoticed. His talent has nearly always been in rendering what one journalist called the mental and emotional paralysis induced by contemporary urban living. "We wouldn't recognize him in the street," he wrote, "because, in a sense, he is all around us."

Robert De Niro once had an idea for a script that told the tale of a young assassin who found himself stalking the United Nations building. The assassin would pick a foreign dignitary out of the crowd and shoot him. De Niro's script idea came six or seven years before *Taxi Driver.* One day, Paul Schrader was sitting with De Niro, discussing the actor's script with him. Recounts Schrader, "I said to him, 'Do you know what the gun in your script represents?' I said it was obvious to me that it was his talent, which was like a loaded gun hidden in him that nobody would let him shoot, and that if somebody would just let him fire once, the whole world would see the enormous impact his talent would have."

VII

Bottled-Up De Niro

In 1975, Bernardo Bertolucci finished filming *1900* just as Martin Scorsese was about to begin filming *Taxi Driver*. In fact, Robert De Niro had just returned from Italy when he stepped into a cab with his renewed hack license in hand. But after shooting was finished, *1900* was to be plagued by many problems before its release in the United States in 1977— chief among them, a lengthy dispute among Bertolucci, the film's producer, and Paramount Pictures over the length of the film.

In the beginning, Bertolucci's producer, Alberto Grimaldi, signed a Paramount contract promising roughly a three-hour film. *1900*'s original budget was $3 million, but as shooting progressed, it exceeded $8 million, and the film became longer than three hours. Grimaldi has said that he protested the zoom in filming costs, but did not want to risk offending the Communist sympathizers of the film crew and the Italian workers in general. "If I had tried to stop production I would have had a terrible mess—riots, maybe."

The running time of the film at the 1976 Cannes Film Festival was five and a half hours. After the showing at Cannes, the director cut the film to five hours and ten minutes. This version of *1900* was split into two parts and released in Italy, France, Denmark, West Germany, Greece, and Switzerland. Business was good but it seemed that less than half the people who saw Part One returned to see Part Two. Bertolucci agreed to cut about forty more minutes of the film, dropping its length to four and a half hours. Meanwhile, 20th Century Fox offered to distribute the film in the United States if the director would only cut a half-hour more. By this time, Grimaldi had prepared a three-and-a-half-hour version of *1900*, without Bertolucci's consent, for Paramount. This provoked a collective outcry from the National Society of Film Critics and the New York Critics Circle, which issued a formal protest to Grimaldi over his plans to release the "unsigned version." Bertolucci condemned Grimaldi and the film that he now disowned. "Two hours cut from a film means the distortion of the language, structure, and significance, and becomes a form of censorship which is an offense not only to the author but to the American audience—which should have the right to judge the work of art as the artist conceives it." The final Paramount compromise for Bertolucci's English-language version of *1900* was a running time of four hours and five minutes.

1900 presents nearly seventy years of history in the lives of two men born on the same day, on the same Italian country estate, at the turn of the century. Alfredo (Robert De Niro) is the son of the landowner and is the estate's heir apparent. Olmo (Gerard Depardieu) is the son of peasants who work the land and whose fate is destined to be the same as his forebears'—to continue working the land with all the other peasant families in return for living on it. As the two boys grow up together, their friendship—an uneasy but enduring one —reflects the changing climate of Italy's social structure: the gradual fall of feudalism, the country's endurance through fascist occupation, and its eventual socialist rule by the end of World War II. *1900* charted the two friends' conflicts, romances, and comradeship through a turbulent period of social upheaval.

Bertolucci describes the film's structure as following the "rhythm of peasant life" and the seasons—starting with summer for the boys' childhood, autumn and winter for the rise of facism and World War II, and spring for the days following the Axis defeat. *1900* is similar to a nineteenth-century novel, the director says, adding that it is a "dialectic" between "American actors and Italian peasants, between fiction and documentary, between prose and poetry, between Hollywood and the red flag," the last in reference to the overt communism of Olmo and the film's peasants.

1900 is a decidedly political film. Did Bertolucci think Westerners would be disturbed by the film's overt subject matter? "Maybe . . . but I don't think so. Everyone who fights for freedom of his country can participate. It's a mistake to focus mainly on one aspect," he has said. "The movie is not a political manifesto. But don't you think it's important that the American audience see the class struggle as human . . . to see that communists don't eat babies?"

1900 provides a lush, elegiac, ochre-colored countryside as the backdrop for the coming-of-age of Olmo and Alfredo. As time and history march on, the two men who should be natural enemies come to understand each other as human beings, although they are on opposite sides of the class struggle. They womanize together, drink together, and even indulge in snorting cocaine together. In one of the movie's lighter moments, neophyte Alfredo is being taught the fine art of snorting cocaine. In a sequence that prefigures a similar scene in Woody Allen's *Annie Hall* (in which Allen sneezes into a jewelry chest full of the white powder), Alfredo snorts the wrong way, sending the cocaine flying off in all directions. This scene shows De Niro in a truly hilarious state of intoxication and demonstrates his gift for slapstick.

But even *1900*'s lighter moments were not able to rescue it or its stars (among them Donald Sutherland and Burt Lancaster) from box-office disaster, though it has since become a cult favorite in revival houses.

Robert De Niro's role as Alfredo did not escape criticism. "De Niro is somewhat overshadowed by a role condemning him to passivity," wrote *Variety*. It was, indeed, the first role Robert De Niro played that was lackluster: as Alfredo, he was a character who almost always makes the wrong choices in his life of privilege; always makes, as one critic put it, "the cowardly choice." He seems to have little "will to power—and his desire not to exercise power led to his capitulation to the fascists." A role of weakness, indecisiveness, and sexual irresolution, as critic Andrew Sarris put it, made De Niro's "smart-ass Americanism" stick out of the lyrical flow of *1900*. Was it Bertolucci's intention to have De Niro's liberal, landed-gentry method characterizations fade to nothing in the scope of the film's propagandistic elements? In any case, Robert De Niro wasn't afraid to risk trying something a little different with *1900.* And neither was Bernardo Bertolucci. Recalling De Niro's early days on the set, Bertolucci says, "The first few days were a nightmare. But I told myself that what I had felt about Bob when I met him was so strong I couldn't have been wrong. I began to try to help him build confidence, and slowly a fantastic actor emerged. The fact is that with Bob you mustn't judge by the first few days. He's a very sensitive and probably neurotic person, so a director can be fooled, but if one has patience, well, it's worth it."

His role as Monroe Stahr, the ill-fated movie mogul of *The Last Tycoon* (1976), was perhaps another such risk. Unlike the bravura characterizations already under his belt, this role would call for restraint and relative calm. De Niro's career would not skyrocket again, as a result of his bottled-up performance in *The Last Tycoon.* Yet, he would deftly bring the ailing, cerebral Monroe Stahr to life.

F. Scott Fitzgerald's *The Last Tycoon* was unfinished by the time he died in 1940. It exposed the passion, glory, scandals, and grandeur surrounding powerful movie executive Monroe Stahr. *The Last Tycoon* was Fitzgerald's first novel that dealt seriously with any profession or business. It chronicled the golden days of Hollywood, a period the author knew very well. *The Last Tycoon* was loosely based on the life of Irving Thalberg, a protégé of Louis B. Mayer. Thalberg was a brilliant, very attractive young studio head endowed with a multitude of gifts. The one gift he did not have, however, was that of a long life. As a boy, a bout with rheumatic fever left him with a bad heart. He would not live past the age of thirty-seven. But during his lifetime, he was a legend. Whether on the dance floor or in the viewing room, he shimmered. "There seemed nothing in his background to account for his gifts or his personality," Irene Mayer Selznick has written in *A Private View.* "Irving was a throw-off, a mutant. . . . The young man with the greatest future in the motion picture business was a man without a future."

F. Scott Fitzgerald met Irving Thalberg during the author's days in Hollywood and worked for him in the fall and winter of 1931. In 1937, when Fitzgerald returned to Hollywood for what would be the final three years of his life, he heard scores of Thalberg stories. Since his death in 1936, Thalberg the late wunderkind had become Thalberg the Myth. In Fitzgerald's novel, Monroe Stahr was depicted as a gentle, frail man. Yet, possessed with enormous skills and insights, he wielded tremendous power. A shrewd workaholic, he was feared and loved by the many people in his paternalistic employ. A nod or a wink from Monroe Stahr could make or break a career.

Robert De Niro's Monroe Stahr was restrained, calculating, brilliant, and flawed—flawed for reasons of health that are never fully explored. He is also bereaved over the death of his wife, the celebrated actress Minna Davis. One night, an earthquake on the studio lot brings about Stahr's encounter with Kathleen Moore (played by Ingrid Boultins), an English emigré with seductive, unearthly charms and intelligence. But her most awesome, chilling endowment for Stahr is her striking resemblance to his late wife. In Kathleen, Stahr finds someone who can extricate him from his weighty responsibilities at the studio, someone with whom, he hopes, he can share his Beverly Hills castle and the oceanfront home he is building in Malibu.

"Bobby has never played an executive, he's never played a lover," Elia Kazan has said. "I had to find that side of him, it was unexplored territory." Before shooting began for *The Last Tycoon*, a memo was issued to the film crew, asking for a professional demeanor on the set. "De Niro works best without distractions," a crew member said, "and Kazan is the kind of director who will do anything to get it [no distractions] for him." For De Niro's role in the film, Elia Kazan did improvisations with him in an office, complete with secretary, assistant, and constant interruption. "[I] impressed on Bobby that what he says is never a comment. Whatever he says is an instruction which someone has to do something about." Dressed as an executive, De Niro walked the halls of Paramount Pictures: "I spent time just walking around the studio dressed in those three-piece suits, thinking 'this is all mine.'"

The interesting thing about Monroe Stahr, De Niro has said, "is that he's able to combine the artistic side of movies with the business side. Usually, they're in conflict. . . . The dialogue is very spare." He says that Harold Pinter, who wrote the screenplay for *The Last Tycoon*, "has the constraint we keep talking about in reference to the character of Stahr. Kazan has more feeling; he's more Mediterranean. He's always trying to play against Pinter's restraint. I think that makes for interesting territory."

During the course of *The Last Tycoon*, it becomes evident that Kathleen is already engaged to be married. Stahr is crushed, yet tries to win her over. His heart failing and his power as an omniscient studio-head challenged by the continuing growth of the Writers Guild and the unions, he becomes depressed. A final, violent confrontation with Brimmer, a young

Communist sympathizer (played by Jack Nicholson) sees his fall from grace in the eyes of the studio's New York stockholders. The last of a dying breed of studio tycoons, Stahr is left to finish his days, presumably alone, amid his riches. This, at least, is where the *film* leaves Monroe Stahr. Fitzgerald's novel ended with Stahr's confrontation with Brimmer.

"Edmund Wilson put together a summary of the rest of the novel from scraps of paper that Fitzgerald had left," said Sam Spiegel, *The Last Tycoon*'s producer. "But I don't believe any of them would have really been incorporated into the book if Fitzgerald had lived. . . . We tried to limit the script to the six chapters he had written, and find the conclusion almost immediately after the sixth chapter: This way you remain faithful to the spirit, if not the entire text, of the book."

The ending suggested in Fitzgerald's notes to *The Last Tycoon* was Stahr's death in an airplane crash—a scene parallel to a suicide at the novel's onset, but not included in the film. Following Stahr's death, according to the notes, would be his glorification with a big Hollywood funeral. The film's ending, with Stahr being dismissed from service following his confrontation with union organizer Brimmer, was invented.

"This is a moving picture that looks at the inside of an interesting person, or complicated person, a confused person, a characteristic person, a gentle person," Elia Kazan recalls. "Monroe Stahr is a good businessman who had an unfulfilled drive to find romance in his life, to expand the boundaries of his life. Here's a guy who was a very tough guy, a great executive, who handles all the problems of his business but who couldn't handle the problems of his own life. When the girl,

Kathleen, became not a romantic figure but a real person, a down-to-earth girl, he didn't know what the hell to do. That's what got him, that's what did him in. I tried to make Stahr ruthless at times. Other times, when he is with Kathleen, he doesn't know, he's uncertain."

Producers like the fictional Monroe Stahr no longer exist, Kazan has said. He was "the last of a kind that tried to make pictures that occasionally lost money, that kept a certain prestige for pictures and, at the same time, kept the general level of his profits high. His methods of production and his tastes became outdated."

Sam Spiegel has compared Robert De Niro to Marlon Brando. "I think it's Bobby's uncertainty about himself that people relate to. He has a quality of searching for his own identity. Marlon had that in his early thirties, when we made *On the Waterfront.* He had an indefiniteness of interest. They used to say he mumbled, but he didn't really, he was just searching."

For the role of Monroe Stahr, Spiegel solicited three actors, all of whom bore a resemblance to Irving Thalberg—Dustin Hoffman, Al Pacino, and Robert De Niro. Pacino never responded to the script, which was sent by Harold Pinter. Spiegel sent another script, and still no answer. Finally, the producer asked a friend who knew Pacino to call him; and an associate of the actor called to say the script wasn't right for Pacino. "Thank you," said Spiegel. "At least you had the decency to call." Dustin Hoffman did call and wanted to talk about the part. However, he was ultimately too busy producing a play on Broadway and filming *Lenny.* Robert De Niro answered immediately and said he would be delighted to do the picture, but not until he finished Bertolucci's *1900,* which was scheduled to finish in two months. Says Spiegel, "So I waited not two, but six months. But he had also arranged with Mike Nichols to start *Bogart Slept Here,* a Neil Simon comedy, as soon as *1900* was finished. So, a picture that was to start in the spring now had to be postponed till October, and it wouldn't have started then if *Bogart Slept Here* had not been cancelled."

Said Spiegel in an interview with *American Film* in 1976, De Niro, "superb actor that he is, was not suited for Neil Simon's comedy." Simon felt that the casting was wrong, and director Mike Nichols was "dubious about the script. Anyway, everyone seemed pleased to stop the picture after two weeks of shooting."

In *The Last Tycoon* Robert De Niro once again found himself in a role more cerebral than physical, a role where his familiar trademarks of careening energy and many-faced forces were turned inward on a troubled psyche. As the single-minded and possessed Monroe Stahr, he had the challenging role of a dazzling young genius who rarely, if ever, succumbed to burden and whose burdens were neatly internalized. De Niro's Monroe Stahr carried the weight of his dwindling authority and power, the weight of unrequited love, and the weight of his impending death.

De Niro's work habits, his total obsession with finding his character thrilled veteran filmmaker Elia Kazan. "He's the only actor I've ever known who called me up on Friday night after we got through shooting and said, 'Let's work tomorrow and Sunday together.' He's the hardest working actor I've ever met and one of the best guys I've ever met in the business. . . . He is a number of things all at once. There are lots of different people in him. He finds release and fulfillment in becoming other people. Picture after picture he gets deep into the thing. He's found his solution for living at a time like this in his work."

VIII

1977: Bobby and Liza

Martin Scorsese's *New York, New York*, which starred Robert De Niro and Liza Minnelli, was a sweeping drama with music that asked: can a romantic relationship be sustained by two people who are equally talented and ambitious? Scorsese's answer would be "no" in this film, which follows the rise of the solo performing artist after the big-band era of the forties and the fifties.

Robert De Niro played Jimmy Doyle, a crusty, aggressive, fast-talking tenor-saxophone player whose dream of fronting a big band becomes a reality. Liza Minnelli played Francine Evans, the singing USO girl he wins over on V–J Day and whom he ultimately marries. Together, in this salute to the big-band musicals of the 1940s, they take to the road, performing with their band from Poughkeepsie to Peoria, gaining national recognition, making it big. *New York, New York* is also a fond remembrance of a New York City past, a time when talented young people flocked to New York, a time when streets were safe, a time before the nightmarish visions of *Taxi Driver* could ever have been imagined.

"It's really about everything everybody goes through—actors, directors, musicians, writers, everyone," Martin Scorsese said. "It's about the period in your life when you're about to make it; you know you're talented, you know you're this, you know you're that, but you just don't quite make it, not for another four or five years." It's that period, he says, "when your first marriage breaks up; when people who are crazy in love with each other can't live with each other." For Scorsese, *New York, New York* was as personal a film as *Mean Streets* and *Taxi Driver*, personal in the sense that it evoked ". . . my aunts and uncles, and my mother and father, the whole period they lived in, the whole business of ambition and what it does to the love relationship." To be sure, Martin Scorsese borrowed bits and pieces from his own life to make *New York, New York* a universal statement about the conflict between the need all people have for love and their drive for achievement and personal fulfillment.

With De Niro as Jimmy Doyle, Scorsese found the perfect instrument for his expression of the conflict: brash, funny, short-tempered, occasionally mean-spirited, ambitious, and talented, De Niro sidles through *New York, New York* like a serpent. His opening scene with Liza Minnelli in a club on V–J Day is a priceless exercise in improvisation. The street-savvy Method-kid and his Ann Sheridan-like glamour gal engage in dizzying pas de deux that set the tone of their mercurial relationship throughout the film. It is perhaps the longest pick up scene in film history, yet is never boring to watch. Effortlessly and hilariously, De Niro and Minnelli glide from conflict to resolution as they size each other up—De Niro, as one critic put it, undoubtedly aware of the lousy impression he must be making, and Minnelli, wide-eyed and shocked, but nevertheless taken in by this madman in hot pursuit of her. "I don't know how any of us survived it," Minnelli recalled. "It was like a whirlwind—it's the only film where I can't remember sitting down."

"It's fun to play different parts," De Niro has said, "otherwise I wouldn't have any knowledge of these types of people. . . . The main thing with a character is to lock in, to make a choice whether it's good or bad, and not be general." De Niro says that his Jimmy Doyle isn't as mean-spirited and selfish as many viewers have found him to be. "You have to find a good side to all characters, no matter how bad they are. If you saw enough of this guy's life, maybe in a twenty-hour film, you'd see his better side!"

De Niro's model and coach for Jimmy Doyle was George Auld, a veteran of such bands as the Artie Shaw Orchestra and the Benny Goodman Sextet. Although *New York, New York*'s saxophone solos were dubbed in by Auld, De Niro, characteristically, insisted on learning how to play the instrument. "It's incredible, the way he learned," Auld remembers. "The kid plays a good tenor-sax, and he learned it in three months."

"My job is to create the feeling that I'm playing," De Niro said. "I play the same stuff that's in the movie; I have to synch to what Georgie plays. It took awhile to learn; I can't read music, but I got a horn and Georgie taught me how to play phonetically, and I've learned phrasing and breathing, the way Georgie does it." Although he couldn't reasonably expect to perfect what Auld took years to master, De Niro say he had to "create the illusion of doing it, which is my job as an actor. The musical phrasing is as lot like an actor's rhythm and phrasing." Some of the hits of the era included in *New York, New York* were "I'm Getting Sentimental Over You," "Song of India," "Once in a While," "Opus One," and "The Man I Love"—all Martin Scorsese favorites, and all of which, he has said, he has on 78 RPM records. "I was born in late 1942," says the director. "I remember the records and films of the forties from my early childhood. I wanted to relate what that music meant to me growing up and connect that with the reality of the films. . . . New York onscreen was more real to me than New York itself, even though I lived there!"

The hit song from the film, "New York, New York," was written for Liza Minnelli by John Kander and Fred Ebb. "It was written as a 'moment song' for her," lyricist Ebb has said. The song-writing duo wrote and rewrote the song three times before Martin Scorsese was satisfied. " 'It's not punchy enough,' he kept saying." The song has since become an international hit, evoking the Big Apple in much the same way as "I Left My Heart in San Francisco" does the city of the Golden Gate Bridge.

Francine and Jimmy finally do make it big in the film. With Jimmy's stunning sax-playing fronting his band and Francine's gorgeous voice carrying the songs, their future seems bright. While the troupe is on tour in New York state, Jimmy makes a rather awkward marriage proposal, demonstrating that some of *New York, New York*'s funniest moments came as last-minute improvisations. When they arrive at a motel, Jimmy, in a parody of the anxious, earnest lover, proposes to Francine, still unconvinced of his love. Their taxi is about to leave, but to underscore the seriousness of his intent, Jimmy throws himself down in its path. Without a doubt, the amazement etched on Liza Minnelli's face in this sequence stems solely from the fact that Scorsese and De Niro neglected to tell her what was planned. "The changes came constantly," she recalls, "from everyone's imagination and enthusiasm. After awhile we were all running around with tape recorders so we wouldn't lose ideas."

New York, New York was shot entirely in Los Angeles, on film sets chosen for their romantically artificial look—even the proposal scene was shot amid studio snowflakes and trees that were obviously cutouts. "The idea of the picture," Martin Scorsese says, "was to get all the surface elements of a forties musical—the sets, the costumes, the makeup, the completely neat hair when the girl wakes up in the morning—and then make a shift to drama."

This shift comes with Francine's pregnancy and her temporary retirement from the Jimmy Doyle Band. With her departure, the band's popularity drops and the marriage is strained to the breaking point. Arguments become embarrassing public confrontations and often lead to physical conflicts. In one fight, Francine and Jimmy argue in the front seat of a car, and they are interrupted by her sudden labor pains. Later, at the hospital, Francine gives birth to a son, a son that Jimmy is clearly not interested in because he stands between him and any chance he has of reviving his sagging career. His depression becomes pervasive and all-consuming, and he is oblivious to Francine and their son. He finally disappears from their lives.

New York, New York's nightclub scenes were resplendent with the flavor and neon glow of the great New York City clubs. Nightclubs like the Rainbow Room and old Harlem night-spots were dreamily re-created for the film. For a scene in one, called The Up Club, De Niro had to simulate a violent breakdown. He had been drinking bourbon to prepare himself. The cameras were not yet rolling, but in a preparation ploy similar to one he had used for a scene in *Bang the Drum Slowly,* De Niro held out his arms and began to spin in circles. The cameras began to roll and he raged drunkenly into the nightclub. After the scene, he conferred with his director. "Bobby hogs Marty on the set," a fellow actor said during filming. "Marty gives Bobby anything he wants. And what Bobby wants is constant attention—constant talk about his character."

"We see things in the character that relate to our-selves," Martin Scorsese said. "In *New York, New York,* Jimmy Doyle freaks while his wife is pregnant. Both our wives were pregnant while we were shooting. We talked about it." Diahnne Abbott, De Niro's wife, had a small but memorable role in the film, lushly singing "Honeysuckle Rose" in one of the nightclub scenes.

In the years that make up the ending of *New York, New York,* Francine Evans forges a successful singing career of her own. Her estranged husband, Jimmy, is a relatively unknown, though fondly remembered, for-mer band leader. He dabbles in contemporary music. One night, after Francine performs the song "New York, New York"—the song whose melody Jimmy had composed years earlier and whose lyrics Francine wrote—the two meet in her dressing room. For a mo-ment it seems that a reunion is possible. They agree to meet later in the evening, at the stage door. He waits outside, but she never appears—she waits inside, but *he* never appears. It is a familiar, unconscious standoff between the two—and a definite departure from the happy endings of the old Hollywood extravaganzas to which, up until now, *New York, New York* has paid homage.

As might be expected, each star of *New York, New York* brought the trademarks of his or her own style to the set of the film. Liza Minnelli's room, on soundstage 29 at MGM, was once occupied by her mother, Judy Garland. Cluttered and filled with flowers, the room and its star were busily attended to by the Minnelli entourage, many of them taking care of her nutritional and personal needs. She was personally picked by Martin Scorsese for the picture. He says, "You can always say 'great, terrific, incredible,' about someone and nobody believes you. But with her, it's true. She's always there with ideas and they're good. It's what I want." Speaking for herself, Miss Minnelli said that *New York, New York* was "an exhilarating experience . . . we had the best of everybody—Bobby, Marty, and the rest. . . . Bobby and I have one thing in common," she says. "We're listening actors. Nothing throws either of us. The ceiling could fall through and we'd keep right on. . . . Bobby isn't one to tell jokes, but I can get him to break up fairly easily. He's totally dedicated and very sweet. There's nothing spoiled about him. He never expects a car, or any of that. He's not into a star trip." De Niro is introverted, she says, ". . . in the sense of being quite private. Bobby's got a funny point of view . . . he sees things a little differently. . . . Real-life situations amuse him and he has incredible curiosity. He's always asking questions."

One of the reasons Miss Minnelli was drawn to *New York, New York* was its honest representation of women. "In all those other forties movies, you never really knew about the woman, what she felt or said after going home. Women get angry and swear, and in this movie I get angry and swear. It's a story I can relate to. When the man leaves, it's not her undoing. She has fulfillment in her work." Also, she says, "For the first time in my life I didn't play a kook. . . . I'm just an intelligent girl-woman in the movie. Robert De Niro has the wacky role for a change. And he's incredible. I think he's probably the greatest actor around today."

Robert De Niro brought his customary near-invisibility to the set, occupying, appropriately enough, Greta Garbo's former dressing room. By 1976, when *New York, New York* was being filmed, much was being made of his penchant for privacy and his tendency toward verbal blackout whenever journalists appeared on the set. "It has to do with pals back home in the old neighborhood," the *Chicago-Sun Times* wrote. "It is for them and for what they might think that De Niro takes no chances his words might come out seemingly vain, indulgent, or pompous." Whatever the case, certainly De Niro's heralded concentration and insistence on not breaking character certainly play a part in his silences. Still, some have begged to differ. "I think he's hiding something he thinks may be too weird," a former colleague on the set said. "I mean, he's protecting himself with all that silence. There's some part of him he can't show because he's afraid it's insane. Maybe it's only egomania, maybe not."

Jon Cutler, De Niro's stand-in, has put it this way: "He is unapproachable. Bob is always working. Thinking. He doesn't want to be bothered. When he was playing Bruce Pearson in *Bang the Drum Slowly*, he seemed to weaken and get sick as his character got close to death. I have no problem with Bobby, except when I try to take too much of his time. He hates to break character, even at night or on weekends. . . . It's spooky how much time he spends without speaking. Bobby is such a quiet actor. He's truly nonverbal. He would be a great silent movie star." Once, while on the set of *Bang the Drum Slowly,* Cutler was sitting under the camera where, he says, ". . . I discovered a fascinating fact. If I leaned my head three feet away from the lens, I didn't see very much coming out of De Niro. He looked boring. But if I stuck my head under the lens, I was watching a genius. He was only brilliant when I sat under the lens. Bob is a guy the camera loves."

With *New York, New York,* Martin Scorsese was finally able to realize a fantasy-come-to-film. "I wanted to have some fun. It's hard to do pictures like *Taxi Driver,* awfully hard. Why should people want to go to the movies and be battled over the head and mugged for two hours? Which in a sense is what happens to you in both *Taxi Driver* and *Mean Streets.* More than anything else, I wanted to have some fun with this film. It's the kind of movie I always wanted to direct."

New York, New York received a cool reception when it opened in 1977. Much of it had been cut to placate distributors' fears that audiences would be impatient with its length. Yet, the film had admirers who wanted to see more, not less, of it. In June 1981, *New York, New York* was rereleased at its original length of two hours and forty-three minutes. Critics by the score issued singingly favorable reappraisals. One of the reasons that critics and filmgoers alike were thrilled was the eleven-minute "Happy Endings" production number with Liza Minnelli and Broadway actor Larry Kent. The added segment, the *San Francisco Chronicle* said,

". . . is easily one of the great musical scenes of all time, and serves as an almost mocking, but beautiful, mirror for the whole of *New York, New York.* "

Martin Scorsese had his own reasons for why his film was so successful the second time around: "I think in a sense that the climate has changed and people's thinking has changed and they're beginning to see what the film is about: the relationship of the people. When it first came out there was so much publicity about nostalgia. . . . People were expecting the return of the big Hollywood musical, which is terrific. I love them, but I can't make them. So when you came to that part in the film with two people fighting in a car, and one of them was pregnant, the public just didn't want to accept that. What they wanted was a big musical."

"When Marty Scorsese had to cut out the small 'Happy Endings' number it just killed him," says Liza Minnelli. "I've never seen a director so destroyed. Now to have the picture looked at again, for people to finally get it, for that number to be put back in, is thrilling." When reviews for the rereleased film appeared, Miss Minnelli wrote Scorsese a note: "I just said, 'How 'bout that?' I got a note back saying 'Really.' "

Since then, *New York, New York,* like so many Scorsese/De Niro collaborations, has become a cult classic. It is a film about music, ambition, love, and the divergent, separate-but-equal paths that two musicians take in their search for fulfillment. At once tribute, parody, and drama, *New York, New York* presented Robert De Niro as he had never been seen before.

While shooting *New York, New York,* De Niro was also getting his body in shape in the boxing ring for another Scorsese project, *Raging Bull.* He would also need that rigorous training for the grueling demands of his next film, Michael Cimino's *The Deer Hunter*. In a two-day period during the filming, De Niro would be dropped from a helicopter fifteen times into the River Kwai.

IX

The Green Beret

Nineteen seventy-nine was a year in which the Vietnam war was transcribed from the fresh pages of history to the various byways of the mass market. Television saw the airing of *Friendly Fire;* Michael Herr's book, *Dispatches,* took to the stage with the help of composer/lyricist Liz Swados; Tim O'Brien's *Going After Cacciato* won the National Book Award; Jane Fonda and Jon Voight starred in *Coming Home.* And Robert De Niro starred in Michael Cimino's *The Deer Hunter*—an explosive, controversial film that saw all the rest dissolve and caused De Niro himself to say, "My role in this movie is the best performance I've ever given." With costars Christopher Walken (Nick), John Savage (Steven), and Meryl Streep (Linda), De Niro led *The Deer Hunter* through not-necessarily friendly fire to blazing box-office success.

Divided roughly into three segments, the film follows three friends of Russian extraction—steelworkers from Clairton, Pennsylvania—to Vietnam and home again to face family and disillusion. *The Deer Hunter* is epic in its scope and sharp in its focus on this close-knit group of friends whose lives are forever altered by war. Yet, *The Deer Hunter*, Michael Cimino has said, isn't about war, but about "ordinary people who go through a crisis and come out of it to continue their lives. . . . If you ask me to sum up the entire experience of making *The Deer Hunter*, I would say that the whole enterprise was an act of faith." It was an act of faith that tested the mettle of director, actors, and crew alike.

The film opens with the three friends garbed in asbestos coats and hoods, standing before a fiery torrent of molten steel. Among them is Michael Vronsky, played by Robert De Niro. Michael is the unofficial leader of a group of pals that also includes Stan (John Cazale) and Axel (Chuck Aspegren). Michael is the "control freak" among them—a cool study of strength, will, and benevolent detachment. His quiet, pensive air of judgment and his ability to show grace under pressure will be severely tested in the time to come.

"When I was preparing for this role I spent a lot of time in Mingo Junction and Stuebenville, Ohio, soaking up the environment," De Niro has said. "I talked to the mill workers, drank and ate with them, played pool. I tried to become as close to becoming a steelworker as possible without actually working a shift at the mill. I'd have done that, too, except none of the steel mills would let me do it. They let me visit and watch but not actually get involved. No one recognized me as being an actor during that time. Friends just intoduced me as Bob and I went from there."

It took months of negotiation with U.S. Steel—and

five million dollars' worth of insurance—before Cimino, De Niro, and company were permitted to film near the central blast furnace, actually in a steel plant in Cleveland. On the job, the site was referred to as the "widow maker."

The celebrated wedding scene in *The Deer Hunter* —the last gathering of family and friends before Michael, Nick, and Steven go to Vietnam—takes nearly an hour and neatly cements the bonds of family, friendship, and tradition. Steven is to marry Angela, played by Rutanya Alda, who is already carrying a child. Whose child it is, isn't certain, but it doesn't seem to matter much. Any one of his friends could be the father.

It is at the wedding reception that Michael and Linda (Meryl Streep), who is Nick's girl, engage in a vague but wonderfully awkward and funny flirtation. Here, for the first time, filmgoers see the De Niro/ Streep chemistry at work, as the two fumble for words while stumbling together on the dance floor. They are both interested in each other—have perhaps always been—but as Linda is the girlfriend of Michael's best friend, the possibility of closeness seems out of the question. In the din of the surrounding celebrants, Michael offers to get Linda a beer. A simple enough offer and, one would think, an easy negotiation, despite a roomful of people. But between the offer and their beer at the bar, De Niro and Streep manage to create a touching, funny scene comically rife with enough "okays," "huhs," and starry-eyed nonsequiturs to fill a movie. They seem made for each other, and at the bar Michael must think so, too: In a sequence that nearly escapes the eye, he leans toward Linda as if to kiss her—then abruptly pulls away.

Robert De Niro and Michael Cimino (in whom the actor met his match as a stickler for detail) travelled 150,000 miles around the continental United States scouting locations for *The Deer Hunter.* They walked around the streets of cities along the Ohio River Valley, and visited steel mills, VA hospitals, and bars. They used the St. Theodosius Cathedral in Cleveland, Ohio, for the wedding scene, used Russian chorale music, real incense, and a real priest. They also engaged actual parishoners from the church's neighborhood for the folk-dancing scenes.

All the domestic locations for *The Deer Hunter* were scouted in the wintertime, but production soon fell behind schedule, and shooting for the scenes in Clairton—actually, Pittsburgh—had to be done amidst the most intense heat wave in Pennsylvania's history. The problem was how to make summer look like winter. All the grass within camera range had to be browned, and leaves had to be stripped from trees. For the actors, the ordeal of filming *The Deer Hunter* was only just beginning. Dressed in heavy winter clothes, they would be drenched in sweat by the end of one take. Meryl Streep's hair had to be continually blown-dry. "This was the most physically exhausting film," Robert De Niro said. The film's deer hunting sequences show Michael Vronsky in his element. Here, the "control freak" with the strength of stone and gazing, pensive eyes communes with the Allegheny mountains. He tries to kill deer with just one shot. None of this can mean as much to his friends as it means to him. He seems to get strength from these mountains, to absorb their granite, gray grace as they fade high into the mist. He seems to make it all a part of himself. And in so doing, seems to tower above his friends.

The Deer Hunter's mountain scenes were filmed 10,000 feet above sea level, on Washington's Mt. Baker. The crew chartered a jet and for three weeks filmed the hunting scenes. As if the incredible change in temperature was not enough to deal with, there was a problem with the deer. "These little deer arrive," Cimino recalls, in an interview with *Esquire*. "I went crazy. The name of the movie is *The Deer Hunter*. We needed big deer. I told them there would be a revolution in the theaters if we killed Bambi." White deer were found on a game preserve in New Jersey. "I had flipped by this point," Cimino has said. "I yelled, 'airship those deer, and I want two.'" Thirty men carried the crates up the mountain.

The crack of a rifle shot shifts the scene abruptly to Southeast Asia, with Michael narrowly escaping death as villagers are killed by enemy forces. The scene is bloody and gruesome. Michael is presently joined by Nick and Steven, and their nightmare begins. They are captured by the Viet Cong and held prisoners in cages partially submerged in a rat-infested swamp. They have been repeatedly brutalized, but the most incredible test of their endurance is about to come. Later, with other Vietnamese prisoners, they are forced to play Russian roulette with a loaded gun as they sit around a table and Viet Cong soldiers wager on their fates. The gun goes round, and Steven is wounded and placed back in a cage. Then, one by one, the Vietnamese prisoners lose, leaving only Michael and Nick. By this time, Nick is beyond panic. He is nearly crippled with fear. He doesn't want to play, but the only alternative is to be murdered. Michael convinces his friend to carry on with their deadly, forced game. Nick places the gun to his head, pulls the trigger. He is saved

—for the moment. It is Michael's turn. He takes the gun, aims it at his head. In a desperate, daring, and swift bid for escape, he turns the gun on his captors and he and Nick overcome them. They remove Steven from the sunken cage and make their bid for freedom.

The Russian roulette sequences in *The Deer Hunter* were controversial not only for their extremely graphic portrayals of fatal wounds, but also because they were wholly an invention of the director. Cimino admitted this, but felt that the scenes acted as a central metaphor for the film. They represent, he said, "men blowing their brains out for money and nations committing suicide in war." As *Time* put it, "The roulette game becomes a metaphor for a war that blurred the lines between bravery and cruelty, friends and enemies, sanity and madness."

The grisly prisoner-of-war scene was one of many in which Christopher Walken got a lot of help from Robert De Niro. "He's the most generous actor I've ever worked with," Walken says. "In the scene where I'm in the gaming room for the first time, for instance and I pick up the gun and hold it to my head, he showed me how to do that. It's a very good moment for me and I have to admit it's stolen." His respect and admiration for De Niro ". . . is one of the things that shows in the film, but it had some bearing on the characters. They're supposed to have been friends for twenty years, there' a powerful feeling between them. I think my feeling about his work helped create an impression of warmth of friendship."

Speaking about some of the violent scenes in th POW camp, De Niro told *American Film* that it wa "very hard to sustain that kind of intensity. I mean, w were really slapping each other; you sort of get worke up into a frenzy. It's a very difficult thing to do. It took a long time."

Following their escape from the deadly gaming room of the POW camp, Michael—again the leader, as he was at home—leads his friends through the tortuous waterways of the jungle in an effort somehow to reach Saigon. Steven is crippled from the waist down and Nick is still traumatized by the roulette game. They try for safe and hidden passage in a flowing river but they are no match for the current. The three are sent hurdling downstream. Suddenly a U.S. Army helicopter appears overhead and attempts to save the three men, who by this time are fixed tightly to a log in the water. After Nick is safely hoisted up, the cable pulls Michael and Steven up to the chopper's runner. Suddenly the two fall back into the cascading river. They are left there to die, yet Michael manages to bring them both to the river's bank and to safety.

The filming of this exciting sequence in *The Deer Hunter* took place in north-central Thailand, near the Burmese border. The location sight was at a spot on the River Kwai. The river was freezing and the air was hot. Local villagers, fearful that something terrible might happen, advised Michael Cimino to build a small Buddhist temple by the river, and they advised him to pray. While working at this location, a revolutionary party— led by the military—seized power in Thailand in a bloodless coup d'état. The filmmakers immediately contacted the new government to gain assurances that the company was in no danger. The Revolutionary Committee promised full protection for the film company and gave assurance of continued cooperation and support for the film.

Perhaps one of the most spectacular—and, for a

moment or two, horrific—events during the shooting of *The Deer Hunter* occurred when De Niro and John Savage elected to perform their own helicopter jump stunts. After getting pointers from stunt coordinator Buddy Van Horn, they climbed onto the runners of a hovering helicopter and were carried up over the River Kwai at a height of about thirty feet. Then they let go, dropping and disappearing into the swiftly moving current below. This feat was performed fifteen times in two days. It almost resulted in their deaths—and Cimino's—when at one point the helicopter's runner got caught in a bridge cable. "We were coming at the bridge," Cimino told *Esquire.* "It had been raised a little so the helicopter wouldn't have to fly so low. The two runners slipped under the steel cables that held the bridge. What that meant was that as soon at the chopper lifted off, it would pull the whole bridge up. The chopper would go down and everybody would be killed." John Savage screamed at the Thai pilot—who couldn't understand a word of English—and the helicopter started careening to one side, throwing De Niro and Savage along with it. "Drop!" yelled De Niro, and they did, into the muddy torrents of the River Kwai. Fortunately, they were rescued by motorboats. The stunt coordinator freed the helicopter from the bridge's cable and all onboard were saved. Cimino's little Buddhist temple was a short distance from where all of this occurred.

Saved, but somehow separated from Steven, Michael finds himself in Saigon. Curiosity has drawn him to a gaming room where the deadly Russian roulette is played for money. He suddenly catches a glimpse of Nick who, since their separation, has been institutionalized at an Army hospital and finally released. Nick is a blank, a cipher. He seems to register little except for the immediate concerns of the game in progress. He is ultimately whisked away by a French colonist. The next time he and Michael cross paths will be after the fall of Saigon.

Michael returns to Clairton a Green Beret hero, a "victor" from a war that, so far as he knows, may have claimed the lives of his two best friends—and altered his way of seeing things forever. The welcome banners have been hanging for weeks, in anticipation of their safe return. Yet, somehow, Michael cannot walk down the main streets of Clairton. The town's storefronts, the old bar, even the imposing steel mill seem alien, trivial in the face of the overwhelming experience from which he has just emerged.

De Niro is majestic, sublime in his alienation here, evincing grace under pressure and control in face of the fact that his old friends haven't changed—that they don't know, perhaps can never know, what he's been through. His hero's welcome is a chilling one for him. The familiar smirk (from *Mean Streets* and from *Taxi Driver*) is intact, but he seems condemned not to enjoy, never to enjoy, his homecoming.

"When Michael reenters the fire of Vietnam, in search of Nick," wrote the *Film Library Quarterly*, "he is playing out a fantasy which flashes in the mind of many Vietnam veterans . . . the survivor guilt fantasy, the desire to go back and bring through combat buddies who didn't make it." And when he finally encounters his friend, and they play the deadly Russian roulette game in which Nick loses, "the capturers, the torturers are Michael and Nick's own minds. Nick dies in the trap of eternal return."

In *The Deer Hunter*'s final scene, after Nick is buried, the survivors come together over a communal breakfast in the bar where they all spent so much time in happier days. Their singing of "God Bless America" seems to affirm their community. They are survivors and, having endured the pain of survival, are no longer young, no longer naïve.

Michael Cimino's *The Deer Hunter* was released across the country on February 16, 1979. However, in a deliberate attempt to qualify for The New York Film Critics and National Society of Film Critics' Awards, the film first opened, for a limited run, at New York's Coronet Theatre on December 15, 1978. It also opened in Los Angeles in December of that year in order to qualify for the Academy Awards.

Universal Pictures was aware that it was taking a risk, that New York critics might have thought they were being steamrolled. "We are taking that chance," a studio executive said at the time, "because *The Deer Hunter* needs awards and the credentials of reviews. If we open in New York, we will get reviewed by *Time, Newsweek,* and the other national magazines. Good reviews will help the film to be taken seriously by the Academy."

The Academy took *The Deer Hunter* seriously enough to award Oscars to both its director and to Christopher Walken, as best supporting actor. De Niro and Streep also won best actor and best supporting actress nominations. Hours earlier, outside the Los Angeles Music Center, Academy members were handed pamphlets that denounced the film as "a racist attack on the Vietnamese people." Articles appeared around the country that called the film "a lie," "a criminal violation of the truth," and a "horrific history" in which all non-Americans were sweaty, crazy, vicious, and debauched. The Soviet newspaper *Izvestia* responded to the film's Academy Awards by accusing it of portraying a war where "the aggressors and the victims changed places."

Many of the film's critics were disturbed that *The Deer Hunter*'s central, bloody metaphor was an invention of Cimino's. According to *The New York Times*, a random check of filmgoers who were deeply affected by the movie found that many of them were upset that the Russian roulette sequences were entirely fictional. "The rising backlash against the movie," the *Times* wrote, "may come partly from the increasing knowledge that the seemingly realistic sequences of violence are not based on any reality."

Speaking in defense of the film and its bloody metaphor a Universal executive said, "Of course that specific incident didn't happen. It's a *film*, and films use metaphors. I'm proud of the movie . . . and I know Cimino didn't intend the movie to be racist. His thrust was to make a film about comradeship among the people who volunteered to fight our wars."

Unprecedented in its graphic depictions of the cruelty of war, *The Deer Hunter* provoked wide and varied reactions. Yet its star, Robert De Niro, was sufficiently impressed with its script to want to do it. "I really didn't want to do anything until *Raging Bull*. But I liked the story and the dialogue. It was so simple. It seemed so real to me." Did filming of the movie test even the humanity, calm, and sanity of Michael Vronsky? "We were risking our lives," says De Niro. "You want it to look authentic, but it is a movie. You don't want to be a jerk about it. It just got all confusing."

During the filming of *The Deer Hunter*, actor John Cazale was dying of cancer. By the time of its completion, the promising young actor, who was engaged to Meryl Streep and who had gained critical acclaim in *Dog Day Afternoon* and *The Godfather, Part II,* had died.

De Niro's next film, *Raging Bull,* would compromise his body and his health. But he wouldn't be taking life-risking plunges out of helicopters or submerging himself for hours at a time under five feet of swamp. He would, however, see himself submerged in sixty extra pounds of flesh for his explosive portrayal of boxing champion Jake La Motta, in a film that would see him win his second Academy Award.

The mild-mannered Jon Rubin of Brian De Palma's *Greetings*, 1968. *Movie Still Archives*

Robert De Niro returned in 1970 in De Palma's *Hi, Mom!* With him here, co-star Jennifer Salt. *Movie Still Archives*

Bloody Mama Shelley Winters and addict son Lloyd Barker (De Niro), 1970. *Movie Still Archives*

De Niro played thieving bicyclist Mario in the 1971 film *The Gang That Couldn't Shoot Straight.* With him here, co-star Leigh Taylor-Young. *Movie Still Archives*

De Niro hit a grand slam as Bruce Pearson, pictured here with co-star
Michael Moriarty as Henry Wiggen in 1973's *Bang the Drum Slowly*.
Movie Still Archives

That's *Mean Streets'* Johnny Boy behind the gun, with David Probal as Tony, 1973. *Movie Still Archives*

De Niro in 1974 on the set of *The Godfather, Part II,* with director Francis Ford Coppola at the camera. *Pictorial Parade*

The young Vito Corleone (De Niro) on the set of *The Godfather, Part II.*
Pictorial Parade

Robert De Niro's performance in *The Godfather, Part II* was a cool, calculated ascent to power—and the Academy Award. *Movie Still Archives*

GF-II-587a-3

Robert De Niro attends Bruce Springsteen's Hollywood debut in 1975 at Los Angeles' Roxy Club.
Frank Edwards,
© *Fotos International*

De Niro and girl friend Diahnne Abbott in 1975. The two married a year later. *Frank Edwards,*
© *Fotos International*

The low-profile De Niro, pictured here at a Hollywood party in 1975.

Frank Edwards, © Fotos International

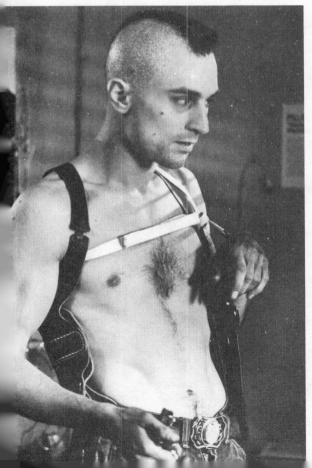

Travis Bickle (De Niro)
strolls with Iris (Jodie Foster) and friend (Garth
Avery) on the mean
streets of *Taxi Driver* in
1976. *Movie Still Archives*

"Are you talkin' to
me . . . ?" *Movie Still Archives*

The dynamic duo: Robert De Niro and director Martin Scorsese during a *Taxi Driver* press conference, 1976. *Frank Edwards,* © *Fotos International*

De Niro and wife Diahnne Abbott at the New York Film Critics Awards, 1977. De Niro garnered the best actor award for his riveting portrayal of Travis Bickle in *Taxi Driver.*

Tim Boxer, Pictorial Parade

De Niro as the ill-fated movie mogul Monroe Stahr, with co-stars
Jack Nicholson (as Brimmer) and Theresa Russell (as Cecilia Brady)
in *The Last Tycoon*, 1976. *Movie Still Archives*

1900 saw De Niro as ambivalent aristocrat Alfredo, pictured here
with co-star Dominique Sanda (as Ada). *Movie Still Archives*

Two musical, mercurial lovers: Francine Evans (Liza Minnelli) and Jimmy Doyle (Robert De Niro) in *New York, New York,* 1977. *Movie Still Archives*

De Niro and wife Diahnne Abbott on "The Mike Douglas Show" in 1977. *Movie Still Archives*

With Meryl Streep in 1978's *The Deer Hunter.* *Movie Still Archives*

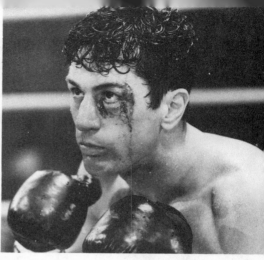

As middleweight champ Jake La Motta in 1980's *Raging Bull*. Movie Still Archives

De Niro and Cathy Moriarty: the future Mr. and Mrs. Jake La Motta, puttering around on their first date.
Movie Still Archives

De Niro won an Oscar for his 1980 metamorphosis of Jake La Motta in *Raging Bull*. With him here is best actress Sissy Spacek at the 53rd annual Academy Awards, March 31, 1981. *Frank Edwards, © Fotos International*

Divided brothers Monsignor Desmond Spellacy (De Niro) and Detective Tom Spellacy (Robert Duvall) in *True Confessions*. *Movie Still Archives*

Two kinds of (dark) comedy share a laugh: Jerry Lewis as Jerry Langford and Robert De Niro as Rupert Pupkin in *The King of Comedy*, 1983. *Movie Still Archives*

The best of friends: De Niro as "Noodles" Aaronson and James Woods
as Max in Sergio Leone's *Once Upon a Time in America,* 1984.
Movie Still Archives

Robert De Niro and
Meryl Streep in 1984's
Falling in Love.
Movie Still Archives

With Jonathan Pryce in
the forthcoming
Brazil. Movie Still Archives

X

Bronx Bully

"Now sometimes at night, when I think back I feel like I'm looking at an old black and white movie of myself. Why it should be black and white I don't know, but it is. Not a good movie, either, with gaps in it, a string of poorly lit sequences, some of them with no beginning and some with no end." So wrote Jake La Motta in his autobiography, *Raging Bull.*

He was called the Bronx Bull and for nearly fifteen years he whipped his adversaries in the ring with an energy and style that, since 1954, haven't been matched. Jake La Motta was born and raised in the slums of the Bronx, the son of Italian immigrants. The first things he learned in life were how to steal and how to fight. He learned, too, that in order to survive the mean streets of New York City he had to be stronger and quicker than the other guy. By nature a loner, he slugged his way through life—and through marriage, friendship, and mobsters who kept the championship title out of his reach. His misanthropy in life, however, made him a winner in the boxing ring. He fought, lost to, and finally beat Sugar Ray Robinson. He wrestled the middleweight championship from Marcel Cerdan, and then lost it, to Robinson. "I fought people nobody else would fight, and in those days, that meant black fighters. I beat them, they were good, but I beat them."

In the ten years Jake La Motta was on the sports scene, he earned millions of dollars—and all of it went for women, houses, cars, and untrustworthy friends. On one occasion, he took orders from mobsters to throw a fight to Billy Fox. "I couldn't get a title match. He had no manager. I was told if I lost to Fox, I'd get a shot at the title. I was offered $100,000, but I turned that down. All I wanted was a shot at the crown." By 1954, his ten years of celebrity came to a crumbling halt. "I opened a nightclub in Miami Beach and got in a row for having a young girl procuring for me on the premises. I served six months on a chain gang." Afterward, he worked at various jobs as a construction worker, garment center employee, contractor, nightclub performer, and a bit player in two films, Peter Savage's *A Home in Naples* and *Cauliflower Cupids*.

With Savage and Joseph Carter, La Motta then wrote *Raging Bull*, a saga of his youth, his rise to fame, and his subsequent public humiliation. It has been called a book that illustrates how the American dream can become corrupted, and how the everpresent lures of wealth, fame, and luxury interfaced with La Motta's own legacy of brutality. In his book, La Motta becomes a metaphor for redemption. And if Martin Scorsese had seen the book first, his ears would surely have stood up. The terrain of redemption and Italian-Catholic guilt had proved fertile ground for many of his films, chief among them, *Mean Streets.*

Robert De Niro was in Sicily filming *The Godfather, Part II* when La Motta's autobiography was sent to him. "There was something about it—a strong thrust, a portrait of a direct man without complications. Something at the center of it was very good for me. I felt I could evolve into the character." De Niro, in an interview with *American Film,* also recalls, "I was interested in fighters. The way they walk, the weight thing. . . . I wanted to play a fighter—just like a child wants to be somebody else. The fun of it is when you get into just experimenting. If you're lucky, you make good choices that will work. As Stella Adler used to say, 'Your talent lies in your choice.' "

De Niro took the book to Martin Scorsese, who had just finished filming *Alice Doesn't Live Here Anymore* and was preparing *Taxi Driver.* Scorsese acquired the film rights and sent the book to Mardik Martin, his college friend from N.Y.U. days and a screenwriter who had worked on *Mean Streets.* By the time Martin handed a script over to Scorsese, the director and Robert De Niro had embarked on *New York, New York.* "I was doing five, six things at once and couldn't give Mardik any input," Scorsese recalls. The script was shelved until 1977, when De Niro and Scorsese finally looked at it. The two called in *Taxi Driver* writer Paul Schrader. "Eventually," Scorsese has said, "Bobby and I did our own version anyway, taking off on the foundation Paul gave us. . . . We knew what kind of film we wanted to make, so we went off to prepare it." It was off to the Caribbean, to Saint Martin for ten days. Here, the character of Jake La Motta would be fleshed out and shaped in detail.

"He would be a street fighter, a street brawler," Scorsese has said. "Norman Mailer once said that Jake was underestimated as a fighter, underestimated as a man. I understand that several sportswriters have said we've glorified a fight-fixer. There is no glorification, and whether he fixed a fight or not doesn't matter. What we had is a picture of a man who didn't compromise." To call *Raging Bull* a boxing picture "is ridiculous," Scorsese remarked. "It's sports but it's something to do with living. Jake La Motta takes on aspects of everybody."

Robert De Niro took on the aspects—all the aspects —of Jake La Motta in the role that would win him an Oscar in 1980. For the celebrated fight scenes he trained with the former middleweight champion for a full year, mostly at New York City's Gramercy Gym on Fourteenth Street. "One year to the day we trained, everyday," La Motta has said. "I guess in the first six months we boxed a thousand rounds, a half-hour straight every day. He wouldn't train unless we wore headgear and mouthpieces, because he knew he was starting to get through my defenses."

The first thing that La Motta taught De Niro was how to protect himself, how to become an expert at blocking. "I taught him not to hold back. I can take a punch better than anybody in the world. I knew how. Then we started working on my style." La Motta's "style," as De Niro recalls, was "crab-like, getting rooted to the ground. . . . Jake would get so low to the ground, very low, and keep moving in, then he'd corner his opponent." It wouldn't be long before De Niro would corner his coach. According to La Motta, he suffered "from black eyes and my upper teeth caps were busted, cost United Artists $4,000 to get them redone.

And there was surgery on my chin after Bobby hit me once, cost $500 or $600. I also fractured a rib, but that's an occupational hazard. I guess I'd rank Bobby in the first top 20 middleweights, I swear."

Interviewed on the set for *Raging Bull,* De Niro spoke excitedly about his transformation to a middleweight contender. "I gained about twenty pounds for Jake and I'm still puttin' it on. I see so many fight movies where the actors are out of shape, I don't believe them. So I come to the gym here—they rigged up a special one—and work out every day. . . . I've got Sylvester Stallone's trainer."

De Niro spent a great deal of time with La Motta out of the training ring as well, practically moving in with him and La Motta's now ex-wife, Deborah. "As a teacher he was very good," De Niro says. "He was patient. He wanted it to be right. He'd tell me when it was off. We had a good relationship. He had a remarkably high tolerance. He never got angry." If anyone was angry it was Deborah La Motta, who during her divorce proceedings, complained to the press that "De Niro was in the apartment constantly for nearly two years." She also said that she thought De Niro's presence may have been a cause of the break-up of her marriage.

For his research on his subject, Robert De Niro also went to Florida to see Vicky La Motta, the second of La Motta's three wives. He saw home movies of Jake, Vicky, and their children—films that inspired *Raging Bull*'s only color sequences and that served as a chronological bridge in the movie lives of the couple. In an interview with *Playboy* in 1981, Vicky La Motta recalled the experience, and recalled, too, that De Niro was acting so much like Jake that it seemed logical to make love to him. "I wanted to," she said. "In fact, I thought: How could I not? An affair seemed the most normal thing to do. But Bob wanted things to be businesslike. I should have just attacked him or something. But I got shy. If I were just attracted to him sexually and didn't like him, I would have known just how to make it happen. But I was intimidated and did everything wrong."

La Motta, aware that De Niro and Scorsese interviewed Vicky, said, "This Scorsese and De Niro, they're sticklers for the truth. I didn't particularly like it. Vicky told me, 'Jake, I know you feel bad about the movie, but it was the truth.' I got to admit that. I was a cruel person. That's what I'm trying to bring out. But it's not the way I am now."

The Jake La Motta of Martin Scorsese's *Raging Bull* is as much a misanthrope as the man himself. Whether trashing the dinner table because his wife burns a steak or mashing an opponent's face because his wife finds that face pretty, De Niro's La Motta swaggers across the screen, exultant. He is fueled by guilt, jealousy, gluttony, and pride. His brilliant career is orchestrated by his brother/manager Joey (Joe Pesci), a sort of cross between Lou Costello and Moe Howard, who lives vicariously through Jake. Joey arranges the fights, is Jake's public relations man, and Jake's third eye, to keep watch on Vicky, a stunning platinum blonde played by Cathy Moriarty. In one of *Raging Bull*'s less violent scenes, Joey assaults a mobster, whom he thinks is coming on to Vicky, by slamming a taxicab door, over and over again, on his leg, which is half in, half out of the cab. Later, Jake, in a jealous rage, beats his brother because he thinks Joey has slept with Vicky.

The film charts La Motta's wins and losses, his highs

and lows, making no attempt along the way to try and explain his tortured, disruptive psyche. He is an unanchored vessel, adrift; or a whirling dervish, flailing out at friends and family alike. "Is he *The Hairy Ape?* I don't know," says Martin Scorsese. "I don't know if he's the noble savage or if he's out of *Of Mice and Men.* It's too easy to categorize things. That's the easy thing to do. Everybody wants to categorize everybody else. That would be a mistake in Jake's case." The characters Scorsese and De Niro bring to the screen seem to have little or no control over their motives. They veer this way and that, almost for want of anything else to do with their visionary (or destructive) energies. They seem to have no choice in the matter.

It would seem that actor Joe Pesci had no choice in the matter of his portraying Jake La Motta's brother, Joey. Robert De Niro had his eye on him after seeing Pesci in the 1970 film *Death Collector,* a movie not unlike *Mean Streets,* in which he played "a crook, a wise guy, loudmouth," and, ironically, a film for which he felt "really overlooked."

The son of a father who pushed him into show business at age four, Pesci was a regular, along with Connie Francis, on NBC's *Startime Kids* by the time he was nine. By eighteen, he was working in nightclubs. Yet, he says, "All my life, everything failed. I had all these chances. The records, the singing. Nothing. My second marriage was breaking up, and I decided to quit show business." Sometime later he became the manager of an Italian restaurant in the Bronx. And one night, Robert De Niro called. He had seen Pesci in *Death Collector* and wanted him to read for *Raging Bull.* He and Scorsese even came to the restaurant to try and persuade him. "My door was open. I had the taste again . . . for a couple of months, I kept reading and reading." When Pesci discovered that at least one other person was also reading for the part of Joey he became angry. "I got mad. I told them I wasn't reading anymore. I said, 'Here's your script, if I can't play Joey, get yourself another boy' and I walked out." He got the part.

"We knew Joe was the one," De Niro recalls. "We did see another kid, but Joe was strong. We saw Joey as mean, just as mean as Jake, not just a poor little brother. It was important and we knew Pesci was the one. Some people have the instinct, the service of truth. Pesci has that." Henceforth, De Niro and Pesci spent all their time together. "We got like brothers," Pesci says, "and it wasn't fake. We're still good friends. I told Robert, "You've got to help me,' and he's kept his word."

An early scene in the La Motta kitchen called for Joey and Jake to engage in a little brotherly roughhousing, which resulted in Pesci getting a little bruised around the ribs. "Just hairline cracks, not broken or anything," Pesci says. "Robert felt terrible. Every take, I made him hit me harder. I had protection but he still hit me right under the heart." For his taxicab doorslamming scene, Pesci did some real kicking and slamming. "I can't stand anything fake. Frankie (Frank Vincent) had pads on his knees and rib cage, and I tried to aim for them, but I'm sure he got a few lumps. It's awkward, clumsy stuff."

Perhaps the most beautiful presence in *Raging Bull* was nineteen-year-old actress Cathy Moriarty, a complete unknown, whose photo was spotted by Joe Pesci at a disco in Mount Vernon, New York. "She's a dead-ringer for Vicky La Motta," Pesci thought. He arranged for her to meet De Niro and Scorsese. "For three months I would go down to the city to read for them," Moriarty, a Bronx native, says. "It was like taking private acting lessons. They never once said that I had the part or anything, and I know they were seeing other actresses, too. I was just happy to be learning about acting from two of the best people in the business, Bobby and Marty."

Cathy Moriarty learned from Robert De Niro how actually to become Vicky, how to stay in character as Vicky. "It was easy, because he was Jake all the time, and then I'd be Vicky. Since he felt it so much, I was able to feel it, too."

She was chosen for the part of Vicky La Motta, she says, because "I fit the role, I fit the character. The real Vicky had a deep voice and a Bronx accent, and so did I. And they also wanted someone whose reactions would be natural and real, and I think the fact that I had never acted before helped me to be that way." The real Vicky La Motta left her own life at the age of fifteen to be with Jake. "When I was fifteen," Miss Moriarty says, "I wasn't fifteen, if you know what I mean. I was a little wild. I wasn't calm; I was adventurous."

Both Miss Moriarty and Joe Pesci were suited perfectly for the needs of Scorsese and De Niro: they were nonprofessional, unconventional actors who blended beautifully with *Raging Bull*'s overall style and design. Cathy Moriarty had "a way, an instinctive way with simple repartee that is totally natural," De Niro says. "She was totally natural even if we were doing nothing. So many actors feel they're not doing enough if they're not walking around." "She was comfortable," Martin Scorsese says. "We'd do a scene, and if it was comfortable it was a take. She was so at ease it was incredible." Miss Moriarty's role as Vicky La Motta raised more than a few critical eyebrows. Vincent Canby wrote in *The New York Times*, "Miss Moriarty comes across with the assurance of an Actor's Studio veteran. Either she is one of the film finds of the decade or Mr. Scorsese is Svengali: Perhaps both."

After most of the scenes for *Raging Bull* were shot —with all of the fight sequences out of the way—cast and crew shut the set down for four months. Robert De Niro's Jake La Motta needed to undergo further metamorphosis if he was to portray the obese, self-destructive Jake of the 1960s; De Niro would have to add sixty pounds to his 160-pound frame. In *Raging Bull*, the audience sees the gradual transformation of La Motta, as De Niro slowly becomes thicker, fatter around the neck and face. For this contribution to the film, De Niro virtually ate his way through Europe in the summer of 1979. "The first few weeks were fun," he recalls. "I really let loose. I would get up early in the morning. You have to get up early to eat three meals a day. I'd have a big breakfast, a big lunch, a big dinner. I pigged out on ice cream. I went to France and went to all the two-star and three-star restaurants and stuffed myself. I kept using those French Alka-Seltzers. I was in agony but in a week I gained seven pounds." He began to realize more about the burdens of being overweight. "You get rashes on your legs. Your legs scrape together. You feel your weight on your back when you stand up. It was a little like going to a foreign land."

De Niro told *Life* more about his trials as the later La Motta. "A doctor was monitoring my health, and he wasn't too happy about it. I had a little problem with my blood pressure. . . . Then I reached the point I couldn't tie my shoes. I was huffing and puffing, and my breathing sounded strange. . . . My daughter got so she was terribly embarrassed for her friends to see me. After all, I looked like an animal."

De Niro recalled going out to his home on Long Island after the film was finished and his struggle to shed the weight he gained. "I took my son into the bathroom, he wanted to weigh himself. He was thirty pounds, and I remember thinking that I had to lose two of him." By the end of the film, he says, "I was depressed. Part of the depression came from having to gain weight." However, the added weight, he recalls, did not really have an adverse affect on his love life. "I mean, some women never give me a look unless they find out who I am, but, believe it or not, some liked me fat—thought I was a big teddy bear." Filmgoers liked Robert De Niro, both as the taut, lithe, and muscled Jake La Motta and as the obese, dissolute one. His unprecedented transformation for the role is now a classic chapter in film and acting history.

The sequences of the later La Motta were actually used as framing devices in the film. *Raging Bull* is a story told by the wasted Jake, whose overblown face is the first one you see on the screen, and the last one, in the dressing room of a nightclub, preparing to go on stage to read from the works of Paddy Chayevsky, Rod Serling, and William Shakespeare.

Raging Bull is also a film about acting. For in it De Niro pays homage not only to the celebrated Method style, but also to its living icon, Marlon Brando. When he utters Brando's famous "I coulda been a contender" speech in front of the dressing-room mirror, he is, as *Sight and Sound* has said, making a direct comment on Brando's Terry Malloy character from the film *On the Waterfront.* "He embodies all the changes that the Method has undergone since Brando's breakthrough in the 1950s. De Niro has taken Stanislavski's notion of becoming a character literally, and in his most recent films there are only vestigial traces of an actor's performance in his work." De Niro has carried the Brando style "to its logical extreme, to the point where the actor's genius is in his transformation." There is no distance between De Niro and the parts he plays: "The identification is so complete that the distinction between actor and role becomes blurred—he enters a character the way that a somnambulist enters a trance," wrote Hal Hinson in *Sight and Sound*. "I just can't fake acting. I know movies are an illusion, and maybe the first rule is to fake it—but not for me. I'm too curious," De Niro says. "I want the experience. I want to deal with all the facts of a character, thin or fat."

"Bobby came from heaven," Jake La Motta says. "He gave me a whole new lease on life."

Raging Bull received the official nod of the motion picture community, and Robert De Niro was rewarded for his incredible portrayal with the Oscar for best actor in 1980. He turned in ". . . the performance of his career," *The New York Times* wrote. *Raging Bull* was "exceedingly violent . . . and, finally, humane in the way of unsentimental fiction that understands that a life—any life—can only be appreciated when the darkness that surrounds it is acknowledged."

That darkness indeed gave light to De Niro's most extraordinary characterization. *Raging Bull*, Veronica Geng wrote in *SoHo News*, asks you to accept humanity without redemption. Other De Niro films up to this point ask the same thing. *Mean Streets'* Johnny Boy is never redeemed. The darkness that surrounds his life will continue to do so, for, as Martin Scorsese has said, Johnny Boy doesn't die at the end of the film—he is condemned to go on living, which is much harder. Travis Bickle experiences a momentary, bloody catharsis at the end of *Taxi Driver.* There is nothing in him, though, that suggests he won't ever be tempted to clean up the streets again. The awesome, frightening angst he embodies still makes headlines, and the enduring contemporary archetype of the urban vigilante is one that has yet to be fully understood.

"They picked my book to do a fight picture," Jake La Motta says. "They took a lot of footage of fighting. But they didn't use so much. The story is about a man who won a championship who wasn't really a nice guy but it's *really* about three people—a man, a wife, and his brother. That's the way I see it."

But in the story of a man, his wife, and his brother —in anybody's story—the surrounding darkness is a major character and is omnipresent. And when De Niro's La Motta speaks half mockingly, half seriously into the mirror, he gives voice to the ways of darkness. And to everybody who coulda been a contender.

XI

The Sacred and the Profane

In 1948, Los Angeles was rocked by one of the most heinous crimes ever committed in its history. Elizabeth Short, a call girl with movie-star aspirations, was kidnapped, brutally tortured, and then murdered. Her murderer severed her body in half and dumped her remains in a vacant lot. The Black Dahlia murder—so named because the victim had been seen dressed in black shortly before her abduction—launched what was to be the biggest manhunt in the history of the Los Angeles Police Department. Elizabeth Short's killer was never found, and the crime remains unsolved.

Using the Black Dahlia murder as a springboard for its plot, John Gregory Dunne's novel *True Confessions* is the story of two ambitious brothers, one a Los Angeles police detective, the other a priest. *True Confessions,* Dunne has said, deals mostly with what he has called the "three-P generation—the generation of young men who left the Irish slums of Los Angeles and thereabouts and became policemen, priests, or politicians." The novel *True Confessions* is relentlessly funny, colloquial, and street-smart. It is rife with black humor in its treatment of local politicians, corruption, duplicity, the police, and the Roman Catholic Church. The death of a priest in a whorehouse and the grisly murder of a young call girl bring all of these elements together in the novel, and split asunder the novel's two brothers—Monsignor Desmond Spellacy and Detective Tom Spellacy. In the film *True Confessions*, the brothers are played by Robert De Niro and Robert Duvall.

Duvall, an Oscar-winner for his role in *Tender Mercies*, has had a distinguished career in theater and film. He has appeared in *The Great Santini*, *The Godfather* and *The Godfather, Part II*, *Apocalypse Now* (for which he received the Golden Globe award), *THX 1138*, *M*A*S*H**, *True Grit*, *The Rain People*, and *The Conversation*, among other films.

True Confessions director Ulu Grosbard is from Antwerp, Belgium. Among the many stage works he has directed are *The Days and Nights of Beebee Fenstermaker*, *The Subject Was Roses*, *A View from the Bridge* (with Robert Duvall), and *American Buffalo*. His film credits include the recent *Falling in Love* (with Robert De Niro and Meryl Streep), the film adaptation of *The Subject Was Roses*, *Who Is Harry Kellerman*, and *Straight Time*. He resides in New York City with his wife, actress Rose Gregario.

"It's not a detective story," Grosbard says of his film *True Confessions*. "It's a story about two brothers. We tried to set it up in a way that the audience wouldn't be surprised that it wasn't. The murder, for instance, doesn't surface until fifteen minutes into the film. It was a calculated risk to cue the audience to the fact that we were more concerned about relationships." The film was about the sacred and the profane—and the conflict between holy orders and law and order.

True Confessions opens as Detective Tom Spellacy pays a visit to his brother Des at a small parish church in the Southern California desert. It is 1962. It has been a long time since they last saw each other, and they have aged. They seem to have difficulty finding words —*True Confessions* is a film of long silences—and their relationship over the years has been fraught with complications. Even as young boys, Des was the favorite, the most likely to succeed, the pious one—like Abel of Biblical times. What draws them together at this moment, though, has nothing to do with the awkward hostilities, jealousies, and moral ambiguities that characterized their parting of the ways in adulthood and that led to Des's exile to this place. "I'm going to die, Tom," he tells his brother. And with that, *True Confessions* flashes back to the beginning of the end of these two brothers.

As the film credits roll, Monsignor Spellacy presides at the nuptial mass of the daughter of Jack Amsterdam. A former pimp, Amsterdam courts respectability in the community as a construction magnate by building cathedrals, schools, and playgrounds. Des Spellacy, a rising star in L.A.'s Catholic Church hierarchy, is friendly with Amsterdam and does business with him. As chancellor of the diocese, Spellacy has engaged Amsterdam to oversee and execute various projects. Amsterdam has offered to sell to the Church one of his many vacant lots, Rancho Rio, and build a church school on it. At the wedding reception, the Monsignor is seen as a knowledgeable wheeler-dealer, despite his role as spiritual pillar of the community. He knows that the diocese is Amsterdam's third choice for the lot, a piece of property that he just can't seem to get rid of. And he also knows that when it is time for the construction of the school, there is no question who the contractor will be. Anybody who bids against Jack Amsterdam is apt to lose his legs or be found shrivelled up in a clothes-dryer somewhere. Monsignor Spellacy has done business with Amsterdam for some years. With Amsterdam's blood money and dubious, fraudulent integrity, Spellacy has made out pretty well. And the Church has made out pretty well. The diocese is well in the black, the Cardinal is happy, and because the Cardinal is happy, the Monsignor's rise in the ranks, toward bishophood, seems unimpeded.

Robert De Niro's preparation for his role of Monsignor Desmond Spellacy was marked by his well-known dedication. Months before *True Confessions* began filming, he studied and practiced the Catholic Mass liturgy. Because of the film's 1940s setting, he learned the liturgy in Latin. With religious technical advisor, Father Henry Fehren, De Niro scrupulously studied Church dogma—and insisted on rehearsing in the clerical garments he would wear in the film. Director Grosbard recalls De Niro's transfiguration: "By the time he was ready to film, he talked like a priest. He *was* a priest." Father Fehren has recalled De Niro, the perfectionist: "He wanted not only to master the fundamental routines of an ordained priest, but he wanted the sense, feeling and tradition of what the Church was in 1948. He may be the most authentic priest ever seen on the screen. . . . How holy we would be if we worked as conscientiously [as De Niro did for his role] at becoming saints."

Yet, the Right Reverend Monsignor Spellacy seems to have lost touch with his conscience and his true purpose in the Church: to serve the people. His business dealings with construction mogul Amsterdam have contributed to his becoming a man of nearly blind ambition—more an accountant than a priest. He manipulates people like chessmen on a board to suit his needs. He is a power broker. He even arranges an audience with the Pope for Amsterdam and regularly absolves him of his sins during confession. He is oblivious to his hypocrisy, and his dilemma is the dilemma of a Church that has strayed from its flocks, that has placed material gain before spiritual gain.

With the murder of call girl Lois Fazenda, Spellacy's place in the community, indeed, in the Church's universe, is jostled. The investigation surrounding her death is led by the Monsignor's brother, Tom. And, while the murderer is never discovered, Tom Spellacy's hard-nosed notion of guilt by association implicates Jack Amsterdam in her death. Fazenda had rendered her services to him more than fifty times. Amsterdam recommended those services to one Leyland K. Standard, who probably killed her.

The detective's ferocious pursuit of Amsterdam has, more than anything, settled an old score. Amsterdam used to "run whores," and, when Tom was on the take on the vice squad in his early days, he saw his old flame, cathouse mistress Brenda Samuels (played by Rose Gregario), get stuck "holding the bag" for Amsterdam. She spent time in jail while Spellacy was spared the public embarrassment and probable departmental discharge for his part in the incident. This was due to his brother's intervention on his behalf. Tom Spellacy has, at best, a serious grudge against whoremonger Amsterdam. Tom's guilt over the past and his disgust for his brother's hypocritical embrace of Amsterdam propel him to avenge not only Lois Fazenda's death but Brenda Samuel's wrongful incarceration. With the gradual implication of the Monsignor himself, the detective's crusade becomes the stuff of high drama. It seems that the Monsignor, along with the diocese lawyer, Dan Campion, once gave the hitchhiking Fazenda a ride on their way home from a weekend at the racetrack. Campion subsequently had intercourse with her. Ignited to a white hot glow, Tom Spellacy sets out to bring down Jack Amsterdam.

In the startling confession-box scene, Amsterdam —who has tried so hard to become respectable only to find out that Tom Spellacy has it in for him—warns the Monsignor to get his brother off his back. Coughing and dying of cancer, he reminds the Monsignor that "you knew her, too," and calls the Monsignor a hypocrite. If Tom Spellacy frames this rap on me, I will bring you down, too, he says. In the other confessional box, Tom Spellacy has just heard—with unbelieving ears—his brother give absolution to Jack Amsterdam. He is incensed. We're going after him, he tells the priest. No matter what the cost. I don't care if you go down with him, he tells his brother.

Between the two confessionals sits De Niro's Spellacy, tortured. On his left, a man with blood-stained hands from years and years of felonious wheeling and dealing, a man who wants to leave this world remembered for the good things he did: the playgrounds, the churches. On the priest's right, his flesh and blood, his brother. Cain and Abel as children. They are perhaps Cain and Abel again, only they have switched roles. Now it is Tom Spellacy who is doing what he thinks is right, and who will spare no one in the process. He is fueled by many things—his abhorrence of Amsterdam; his lifelong resentment of his brother; his guilt over the suicide of Brenda, whose plea for financial help from Amsterdam was ignored—many things. And De Niro's Spellacy is caught in the cross fire, his moral crises flickering across his face like the flame of a votive candle. It's as though all of his "private moments" were up for auction. Director Ulu Grosbard pays homage to that face, lets it play out its bottled-up ambiguities, in torture, in pain, in guilt; in crisis and resolution. Tom Spellacy doesn't care who he brings down. "Neither do I . . . Neither do I," the Monsignor says.

Toward the film's end, the careers of both priest and pimp are washed up. Tom Spellacy has won his questionable battle, Jack Amsterdam is presumably off the social scene forever, and Desmond Spellacy is transferred to the desert parish, never to be a bishop. It is 1962 again, and Des has delivered his devastating news to his brother: his heart is fast failing, he does not have long to live. Tom offers apologies and accepts the blame for his brother's exile from the community. Des, on the other hand, sees nothing for his brother to apologize about. He absolves him from his guilt and credits Tom with forcing him to relearn the things that power and ambition caused him to forget. Never good at loving God, he has at least tried to make himself useful in this desert parish. The two walk in silence among the headstones of the church's cemetery. Des shows Tom the plot where he wants to be buried and expresses the hope that, when Tom dies, he will lie next to him there.

The concerns of *True Confessions* are many and complex. While on the surface it seems like a potboiler murder-mystery, beneath its rough, grisly terrain are the complicated machinations of an extraordinary, guilt-ridden sibling rivalry. *True Confessions* is also a film about corruption and politics in the usually sealed and sacrosanct worlds of law enforcement and the Catholic Church. "It doesn't have a strong action line," Ulu Grosbard says of his film. "It's an interesting film to follow, though. There are many strands that weave themselves together before it's over." And, he adds, with regard to the murder: "Oh, you find out whodunnit. But it doesn't really make any difference." *True Confessions* is a film about moral ambiguities and hypocrisy, absolution and forgiveness. Not big box-office draws, to be sure, but its stellar blend of ensemble acting, rich with nuance and dialogue, made the movie critically acclaimed and a sure winner for De Niro and Duvall fans alike.

Filmed at about sixty sites in Los Angeles—among them City Hall, Union Station, Chinatown, St. Joseph's Cathedral, and Fort MacArthur's barracks—the screenplay for *True Confessions* was penned by the novel's author, John Gregory Dunne, and his wife, writer Joan Didion. Their other film collaborations are *Panic in Needle Park*, *Play It as It Lays* (based on Didion's novel), and *A Star Is Born*.

Originally, Paul Schrader was tapped to write the screenplay for the film. Schrader wanted to cast Peter Boyle (who played Wizard in *Taxi Driver*) for the role of Detective Tom Spellacy, with Robert Duvall as the Monsignor. Schrader had used Boyle in his film *Hardcore*. But producer Irwin Winkler felt that he could get De Niro for *True Confessions*. "I didn't think he could and I was wrong," Schrader told *Esquire* in a conversation that included John Gregory Dunne. "I wanted to do [*True Confessions*] quite badly, but I had an idea of my own that I wanted to write and I was just arrogant enough to feel that if I could do my own material, I didn't want to do someone else's."

True Confessions is very much an actor's film, parading as it did the tremendous talents not only of its two stars but of the supporting players as well: Charles Durning as Jack Amsterdam, Ed Flanders as lawyer Dan Campion, Burgess Meredith as Father Seamus Fargo, Rose Gregario as Brenda Samuels, and British actor Cyril Cusack as Cardinal Danaher. De Niro and Duvall, wrote Vincent Canby of *The New York Times,* "play together with an intensity and intelligence that illuminates the film as well as the performances of the hugely gifted cast . . . no American film in a long time has presented such conjunction of acting talents . . . here, truly, is the kind of film for which there should be a collective award for all of the performances."

As Monsignor Desmond Spellacy, De Niro brought to the screen an ambitious, powerful, and finally tortured and doomed careerist. Not since *The Last Tycoon* had he engendered such internalized struggle. It was a departure for De Niro, to be sure, from the flamboyant personalities of recent years' work. But like most of his departures, his risks, it won him accolades and enduring respect.

"I want to make things concrete and real and to break down the illusion," the actor says. "There's nothing more ironic or strange or contradictory than life itself. What I try to do is to make things as clear and authentic as possible. . . . Technique is concrete. I don't want people years from now to say: Remember De Niro, he had a real style. I want to do things that will last because they have substance and quality, not some affectation or style because that's all bullshit."

For his next film, which would pair him again with

director Martin Scorsese, he would change from his role as a priest to dark comedy. And alongside the portraits of Johnny Boy, Corleone, Bickle, et al., would hang the desperate, smirking picture of kidnapping comedian Rupert Pupkin of Clifton, New Jersey.

XII

Pupkin Pie

The King of Comedy, released in 1983, is Martin Scorsese's mordant examination of celebrity, stardom, and the lot of an obsessed fan who is also an aspiring star. It offers a sobering look at the offstage life of a celebrity—Jerry Langford (Jerry Lewis)—and a chilling tale of a social misfit—a Borscht-Belt aspiring comic, Rupert Pupkin (Robert De Niro). Pupkin pursues Langford, but fails in his attempts to gain his help and camaraderie. As a last resort, Pupkin kidnaps Langford for a ransom of fifteen minutes on Langford's television show. De Niro's Rupert Pupkin—like many of his celluloid creations—is an outsider, who wants to be publicly acknowledged. Like Jake La Motta, he is surrounded by darkness.

"*The King of Comedy* is a film about the desperate need to exist publicly, which is so American," screenplay writer Paul Zimmerman says of his script. "It's the

ultimate outgrowth of the question 'What do you do?'
. . . The problem Rupert faces is: Will he ever count?
And for him, it is a matter of life and death." Zimmerman was first struck with the idea for his screenplay
after viewing a David Susskind show about autograph
hounds. "I realized that autograph hounds are just like
assassins except that one carries a pen instead of a gun."
In 1974, when director Martin Scorsese read it, he dismissed it as a one-gag film; the story of an aspiring
comic who kidnaps a famous talk-show host in order to
get on television just didn't interest him. Time moved
on, and with it, *Taxi Driver, New York, New York,* and
Raging Bull. When Scorsese finally read the script for
The King of Comedy again, it somehow took on a new
significance for him. Success had changed his life. As
well-known movie figures, both he and De Niro could
relate to the awesome burdens that came with celebrity—the hangers-on whose goodwill sometimes mask
dishonorable intentions; the coattail-riders to success;
personal crises, marriage break-ups. Scorsese also identified with Pupkin's desire for success. "I can identify
with Pupkin," he has recalled. "Pupkin goes about it
the wrong way, but he does have drive. I remember I'd
go anyplace, do anything. I'd try to get into screenings,
get into any kind of social situation to try to talk up
projects. It's important who you meet; after all, if you
meet forty or fifty people, the one person who will
produce your first film might just be there."

The film that Martin Scorsese, Robert De Niro, and
Jerry Lewis finally brought to the screen was much
darker than Paul Zimmerman's original script. "I
wanted to work at what it's like to want something so
badly you'd kill for it," Scorsese recalls. "By kill I don't
mean kill physically, but you can kill the spirit. You can

kill relationships, you can kill everything else around your life." Celebrity, he says "*does* affect personal relationships, and the final line for me *at the time* was that if I had to make a choice between work and a relationship, the personal relationship would go by the wayside."

The King of Comedy opens with pandemonium at the stage door of The Jerry Langford Show. Fans are screaming, waving autograph books, waiting for the celebrity talk-show host to come out. Langford can hardly make his way through the stampede of frenzied fans to his waiting limousine. Suddenly, Rupert Pupkin emerges from the crowd. He is Langford's savior for the moment. He helps Langford, and himself, into the car, and the car drives off, chased by frantic fans. Pupkin, like someone on a first date with a girl, tries to win Langford's friendship. Maybe you could use me on your show, he suggests. Not wanting to seem ungrateful or rude, Langford responds to Pupkin's entreaties with a customary "call my office." More dismissive, of course, than sincere. The remark, nevertheless, triggers Pupkin's manic sensibility. From here on, it is quite possible that the rest of *The King of Comedy* is all Rupert Pupkin's fantasy, all played out in his head. He immediately sets off to make a pest of himself at Jerry Langford's office. For Pupkin knows that there is no doubt about it—he will soon be the "king of comedy."

For his role as the celebrity-crazed Rupert Pupkin, De Niro tracked down a handful of real-life autograph hounds and interviewed them, asking about their lifestyles in star-tracking and in autograph hunting. "De Niro even came out to my house with director Martin Scorsese to see my collection," said Barry Talesnick, who, along with three of his colleagues, played extras in the film. De Niro also prepared for his role by watching young comedians strut their stuff for some very tough audiences at some of New York's hottest comedy clubs. For the actor, the essence of Rupert Pupkin was elusive, difficult to define. "There are some scenes themselves that are funny," he recalls, "but when you try to explain them, it becomes corny. They don't sound like much, sort of like TV comedy." The script, he says, is "very funny, but you have to *listen* to it."

De Niro's co-star Jerry Lewis, he recalls, was a great help in perfecting Pupkin's comedy routines. He was "very good, very professional, he wanted to help everybody . . . he stepped in to help, he connected with our rhythms, most often out of instinct." Martin Scorsese personally selected Jerry Lewis for the role—a role that was originally turned down by Johnny Carson, who feared that it might inspire a similar, real-life kidnapping—and found that Lewis "helped with intangibles like body moves. He knew when you had to be this way. He knows lenses. I came to rely on him, to talk to him. I purposely did long takes on him so I could study him." Scorsese found in Jerry Lewis "such a powerful figure, in the tradition of Keaton and Jacques Tati, and not only in terms of comedy but in terms of an institution."

Jerry Langford, the institution, has to endure the battering ram of Rupert Pupkin who, failing to gain admission to the Langford office, devises a plot to gain entry to Langford's weekend hideaway. Pupkin convinces, Rita (Diahnne Abbott), his former high school cheerleader sweetheart, now a bartender, that Jerry Langford has invited them both out to his country house for the weekend. Over supper in a nearly empty restaurant, Pupkin glamorizes and glorifies his limousine encounter with Langford, gesturing broadly and animatedly—while, behind him, a restaurant patron mimicks his movements. Rupert convinces Rita to join him on the ill-fated trip to Langford's mansion. This will be the ticket to ride, for both of them.

Their visit is an unmitigated disaster. Langford's ire is sufficiently roused to incur Rupert's animosity and Rita, an innocent in all of this, has to endure the humiliation of being Rupert's dupe. As they are ushered out of the Langford estate, she swipes a small piece of bric-a-brac in anger over Langford's rough treatment of them. Dressed in the peach-colored gown she bought especially for their weekend with Jerry Langford, Rita seems to be the only authentic, well-meaning innocent in *King of Comedy*'s harsh, jaded tableau.

With all the "rational" means of propelling himself into Jerry Langford's orbit exhausted, Rupert has only one solution left. With the aid of fellow Langford-fanatic, Masha (Sandra Bernhard), he plots to kidnap the star and hold him for ransom. If Rupert doesn't succeed in getting his TV spot, if the world doesn't sit up and take notice of him, he will kill Langford. Masha and Rupert stake out Langford, wait to see him walking alone on the city streets.

Martin Scorsese and Robert De Niro had been Jerry Lewis fans for a long time. They didn't make it easy for Lewis on the set of *The King of Comedy*. The comedian is used to having directorial star-control over projects with which he is involved. He did not in the case of *The King of Comedy*.

At one point during their collaboration, Lewis told *People*, he asked De Niro to join him for dinner. Typically insisting on remaining in character for his part, De Niro declined. "I wanna blow your head off. How can we have dinner?" he said. In the sequence that required Lewis to explode in anger at Rupert, De Niro began their scene by yelling out anti-Semitic epithets at Lewis, saying that Jews have "turned the world into a garbage dump for 5,000 years." The actor's ploy was successful: "I forgot the cameras were there. At the end, Marty couldn't just say 'cut'. I was going for Bobby's throat!" De Niro, Lewis says, ". . . is an absolute genius. I never knew how much effort he puts into a role. He plays me in the movie and is so much a perfectionist that he wouldn't even socialize with me while we were shooting. He didn't want to get too close to me. But when he was doing a scene, I took off for two days of golf in Winston-Salem, North Carolina. He remembered the watch that I wear and insisted that he wear the same kind to better portray his role."

De Niro, who is well known for fleshing out and refining his roles during a number of takes before the camera, found Jerry Lewis a dedicated fan. "Take one," Lewis told *People*, "Bobby's getting oriented. By ten, you're watching magic and in take fifteen, you're seeing genius." As for Lewis' role in the film, "The less Jerry does, the better he is," says Martin Scorsese. He is "almost playing himself. He's wearing his clothes, his glasses. That's his dog in the apartment. . . . Jerry has done nearly everything in show business. He had a lot to draw on and he was eager to play the part." Scorsese had two meetings with Lewis over the course of a year and a half, before shooting for the film began: "I could see the man was ripe for it," he said. Indeed, Jerry Lewis tossed off the stone-faced, incredulous Jerry Langford with apparent ease.

The film continues as Rupert and his pugilistic pal Masha abduct Jerry Langford and bring him to Masha's spacious East Side apartment. Rupert's demands and conditions for Jerry's release are printed on cue cards and the comedian is forced to read them, at gunpoint, over the phone to his bewildered producers. Convinced that Langford's desperate communiqué is authentic, they proceed with plans to accommodate the abductor. Tony Randall is tapped to guest-host the Langford show, which is to be taped in a few hours for its late-night broadcast. The producers contact the police; Rupert goes across town to tape his appearance, and Masha is left alone to guard Jerry, the only man, who has made her life worth living. She preens over him, singing and dancing around, trying to seduce the bound-and-gagged Langford. It is hilarious. She is alternately a cuddling, protective mom and a voracious, thick-lipped, sexual harpy. Star-struck and redeemed, she hovers over her cornered quarry. This is her moment.

The tour de force role of Masha was played by newcomer Sandra Bernhard. It was a performance that saw filmgoers leap up and take notice of the hitherto unknown stand-up comic. A former manicurist to the stars in Los Angeles, she was surely the queen of *The King of Comedy,* practically stealing the show from both De Niro and Lewis. Of her memorable scene with Lewis, she says, "That was probably the hardest scene. ... Scorsese expected me to improvise within the realm of reality, and I was all over the place. So Jerry pulled me aside to explain that I had really good ideas but I had to put them together." Lewis, she told *New York,* "was an imposing figure. He was bigger than life, like the ultimate dad, everybody's dad. He scared me. And I really did want him to like me in real life as well as the picture. But I think in order to make the scene work he never gave me much attention in either place." As for De Niro and Scorsese, she found them both to be "real down to earth." Of De Niro, she said, "He doesn't strike me as the type of man who has a lot of women friends, but he's great, very giving and unthreatened. If you're going to overpower him in a scene he'll let you. He doesn't have to be the center of the screen the whole time."

After a few hours, Jerry Langford finally convinces Masha to remove the gag from his mouth and, finally, the thick tape that has him bound to his chair. He quickly overpowers her, and escapes from her clutches. Masha, clad only in a bra and panties, chases after him, to no avail. Meantime, back at the studio, the taping is done and "The Jerry Langford Show" is about to air. Surrounded by police detectives—one of them tells him that he should be jailed strictly on the basis of his bad jokes—Pupkin insists on watching his national television debut at a place of his own choosing. Only then, after he watches the broadcast, will he tell of Langford's whereabouts. He leads the detectives to the bar where Rita works and, with Rita and the regulars (among them the director's father, Charles Scorsese, and Mardik Martin, the director's occasional collaborator) watches The Jerry Langford Show. He is vindicated, then arrested and then he is a hero, or, rather, an antihero, who broke the law in a desperate career move. While in prison he writes his autobiography. When he is discharged after two years, he becomes the toast of the town and basks in the bright lights of the celebrity he has craved all his life.

The King of Comedy's ending, whether real or imagined by Rupert, unavoidably brought to many minds the controversial ending of *Taxi Driver*, with Travis Bickle lauded as a hero for taking the law into his own hands. *"The King of Comedy,"* wrote the *New York Review of Books,* "doesn't share a joke with the audience . . . it makes the audience into dupes: if you laughed at Rupert's jokes, you made a criminal a star. And in raising the specter of the controversial *Taxi Driver* ending, it courts more anxiety, and more press maunderings about movie violence . . ."

The King of Comedy was the opening film at the Cannes Film Festival in 1983 and was also chosen the best film in the fifth annual poll of film reviewers, sponsored by the Critics Circle of Britain. A dark "comedy," to be sure, it, like so many of the De Niro/Scorsese collaborations, was autobiographical in its depiction of celebrity and celebrity-chasers. In it, De Niro added another compelling portrait of alienated American flotsam to his gallery. "Better to be a king for a night than a schmuck for a lifetime," Rupert Pupkin says, thereby closing the book on the subject of the uniquely American obsession with instant celebrity. *The King of Comedy* is a reminder, Rex Reed wrote, that "crime not only pays, but has lasting benefits and annuities, like movie deals, book contracts and magazine covers . . . there's no denying the film's lacerating impact as it peels away another layer of the ugliness of American life."

The King of Comedy portrayed the fan as worshipper and menace, one critic wrote, and Rupert Pupkin as the "nice nut, the dangerous devotee, the logical looney who can pop up at any moment with a grin, a gag or a gun." Says Martin Scorsese of Rupert Pupkin's finale: "Sure we give Rupert a big salute at the end and he gets his own TV show, but Nixon got his own TV show, didn't he? He's got one on *Great Men.* And G. Gordon Liddy's got his own show too. Our idea is perfectly in the mainstream . . . it's a dangerous situation. The culture is in danger. What Rupert does is a crime. To reward it is a bigger crime."

Another reason Johnny Carson turned down the offer to star in *The King of Comedy* was that as a one-take television professional he couldn't imagine forty attempts to get a shot. "He further rationalized," Scorsese says, "that if he were to act in a film why should he play himself? But he was very helpful. During shooting we'd call him up and ask questions. Every time we called, he said the same thing: 'What's the matter? You lose Jerry?' " Scorsese says that *The King of Comedy* was ". . . disturbing to make. It's obvious we're not saying this is the way to break into show business . . . it promotes an idea that's absolutely horrible, a complete turnover of values. It's the anger of the situation that prompted me to do the movie."

Time wrote that Jerry Lewis' Jerry Langford ". . . mimes warmth perfectly until you notice the deadness in the eyes betraying the veteran public figure's inability to perceive any reality, even a menacing one, that exists outside his own ego." And as for Rupert Pupkin? Vincent Canby said it when he summed up De Niro's chilling portrait as "one of the best, most complex and most flamboyant performances of his career."

Robert De Niro had some words to say about Rupert Pupkin, and some observations to make about the fact that *The King of Comedy,* while noted as a critical success, failed to make an impressive box-office showing. "When I play a character like that, I'm not comfortable. I feel uncomfortable about forcing myself on people. I don't feel good about it, so I know how that man felt in that situation. . . . I think maybe the reason *The King of Comedy* wasn't well received was that it gave off an aura of something people didn't want to look at or know. Take our presidents. Kennedy gave one kind of aura based on charm, but Nixon had a kind of negative thing going for him. People react to what's projected."

With the addition of Rupert Pupkin, De Niro's gallery of misfits, à la Scorsese, would temporarily be filled. His next film would find him back on mean streets again, gangland style.

XIII

Once Upon a Time...

O*nce Upon a Time in America* saw Robert De Niro in a familiar setting. The rough-and-tumble streets of lower Manhattan served as the backdrop for Sergio Leone's sweeping tale of Jewish gangsterism, beginning with the 1920s and reaching to the late 1960s. De Niro, of course, was no stranger to the streets or to the thematic concerns of the film. As Jon Rubin in *Greetings* and *Hi, Mom!* and as Johnny Boy in *Mean Streets,* he had pounded the labyrinthine pavements of lower Manhattan and had characterized the hoodlums who wheeled and dealt in their neighborhoods. And, of course, in *The Godfather, Part II,* as the young Vito Corleone—a role that won two Oscars for De Niro and Brando—he came of age in the territory of organized crime. It was the old neighborhood of De Niro's real life and his life on the screen.

Leone's epic saw De Niro in the role of Noodles

Aaronson, a tough guy with something of a warm heart. Noodles was a character drawn from two real-life gangsters from Manhattan's Jewish ghetto, Bugsy Seigel and Meyer Lansky. Both were on the scene in the twenties and the thirties. James Woods played Max, De Niro's best friend, a tough guy with a much colder heart. *Once Upon a Time in America* is about Noodles' life of crime, from 1923 to his old age in 1968. "I think these two men," Sergio Leone says, "rather than expressing two different personalities, are like occasionally discordant aspects of the same character." In an interview with *Sight and Sound*, he said, "It's like separating the fundamental aspects of man's nature with a hatchet blow and attributing them to different people and then making them flow together into one story so they can clash, struggle, consolidate and then separate again."

Shot in Rome, Venice, New York, Toronto, and Paris with an international cast, *Once Upon a Time in America* was originally contracted, with Warner Brothers, to run two hours and forty-five minutes. Sergio Leone's finished product was three hours and forty-five minutes. Defending Warner Brothers' contracted length, producer Arnon Milchan said that he felt that American audiences were traditionally resistant to "marathon" films. Also, *Once Upon a Time in America* ran about $6 million over budget, finally costing $30 million to make. Speaking of Warner Brothers' editing of what became the shorter U.S. version of the film, Leone has said: "The relationship I have with them is a relationship of things that have been done. There was no way I could stop their version from being released."

In Leone's version, the story unfolds through a series of flashbacks, all representing Noodles' memories. The flashbacks are not chronological, which is essential, Leone says, because "time is one of the major characters in the film. This film is about memory, nostalgia and death."

Leone's *Once Upon a Time in America* opens in 1933, with a scene in which a young woman, Eve, enters the bedroom of her lover. She pulls back the bed covers and sees the bullet holed outline of her gangster lover, Noodles Aaronson. Suddenly a framed photograph on the table beside the bed is smashed. "Where is he?" an intruder demands. Eve says she doesn't know, and then she is fatally shot. Violence begets violence as three thugs go in search of Noodles. Their search leads them to an opium den, where Noodles is seen for the first time. He is reading a newspaper whose headlines tell him that three of his friends, all Jewish, have been killed in a bootlegging caper.

In a moment we are in 1968 with a paunchy and graying Noodles Aaronson emerging from a thirty-five-year exile, to confront those he has lived in fear of for the past three decades.

Once Upon a Time in America then flashes back to 1923, to the young Noodles and his pals as they play out the small-time thieving and petty misdemeanors that will shape their destinies. The basic plot, then, centers on five Jewish immigrant kids from poor families who begin a reign of terror robbing drunks, blackmailing cops, shaking down small businesses, and, in one scene, burning down a newsstand. Noodles is the leader of this pack of wolves, and *Once Upon a Time in America* chronicles the bloody rise of his gang through thievery, bootlegging, and racketeering. The gang rises, though, while the young Noodles lands time in prison for knifing to death a rival gangster. He returns as an adult to discover his buddies have set up a speakeasy and bordello, in which he is an equal partner.

Noodles' volatile friendship with Max is the shifting

framework of the film. Max grows increasingly destructive and ruthless in his gangland activities, while Noodles, at first his seemingly psychotic lieutenant, becomes mellow and seems indifferent to their life of crime. In his lifelong goal to make the big time, Max concocts a plan to knock off the Federal Reserve Bank. But even his gun moll, Carol, and his best friend see that the job spells doom. It's a life-risking undertaking. With dissent in the ranks, Max sees what he's known all along: his pals simply don't have the right stuff or the desire to break into the big time. Max decides to pull off one last small-time operation—a liquor heist. But Noodles decides to let the police know about the robbery, hoping that a stint in jail—a stint that would include his own incarceration—will sober them all up from the delirious notion that they could succeed in holding up the Federal Reserve Bank. He doesn't realize that his partners in this will all get wiped out in a bloody carnage and that he will become the object of a Mob manhunt.

Noodles flees to Buffalo, where he spends the next thirty-five years in quiet fear of retribution. At the end of the film, Noodles discovers the truth of that fateful night's events. He receives an invitation from a mysterious senator whose career is in jeopardy due to his recently discovered underworld connections. He is invited to a party at the senator's estate, a party the apparently ageless Deborah, the girlfriend of his youth and who is now a famous actress and who is married to the senator, has warned him not to attend.

At the party, Noodles is ushered into the senator's private chamber. The senator turns around to face him. He is Max. Yet Noodles seems to have been prepared for this reincarnation of his friend, quite undead after thirty years and with a new identity. Noodles reveals no surprise as Max offers the details of his deadly betrayal of thirty years past. Max had set up the bloody rub-out with the full cooperation of the Mob, into whose ranks he so desperately sought acceptance. He advised Noodles not to go on that fateful night because he would never have had the courage to kill his friend. Instead, he tried to have Noodles executed in his own bed but failed.

Noodles steadfastly refuses to acknowledge the senator as Max. He wonders why the illustrious senator sent for him, a small-time crook who has been off the circuit for all these years. It's simple, Max says, trying to deny the impervious, unrelenting Noodles. His recent troubles spell the end of his career, his life. There is no way out of the crisis, the investigation, that envelops him. He wants to die. And there is no one but Noodles, the flip-side of his twenty-five-cent cowardice, who can make, who deserves to make, this happen. He offers Noodles a gun, virtually begging him to kill him. Noodles, face-to-face with the reason for his thirty-five-year exile, refuses to kill him. Taunting, never losing his demeanor, he says he is sure that all the senator's problems can be worked out, that once this terrible investigation is over, the senator will be cleared of any charges that tarnish his golden reputation. Tension mounts. Max would pull the trigger himself, but it wouldn't look good. Better to have it appear that an intruder did the deed. He promises Noodles swift and easy escape, through a secret passageway to the street. But Noodles is firm in his refusal, masterful in his denial of Max. He departs through the passageway down to the streets below.

Parked outside the estate is an idling garbage

truck. As Noodles walks away from it, the headlights are switched on. He can discern a figure walking in his direction. The truck starts to move forward slowly. It moves at a growling pace along the street, coming between Noodles and the figure, who is on the sidewalk. Noodles sees the truck slowly pass by the figure. But after it lumbers by, the figure is nowhere to be seen. All Noodles sees is the back of the truck, inching its way down the road, its cavernous guts of twisting metal churning the silent refuse inside. At this point *Once Upon a Time in America* jumps back to the young Noodles in his opium den on the eve of his exile.

Leone's circular epic in its pristine form is a deep inhalation and exhalation of time, memory, and event. These are the themes that rule his version of the film, that take precedence over subject matter. Through the randomness of a life's recollections, the events that shaped the lives in the film are portrayed on a dreamy tableau, shifting and unanchored, as recollections are. *Once Upon a Time in America* demands the filmgoer's undivided attention. Its unconventional structure makes it perhaps the least accessible of Robert De Niro's films. Photographed by Tonio Delli Colli and scored by Nino Morricone, the film draws the viewer into its hard-edged subject matter and then sets him free to float with its other, heady preoccupations.

The Leone version of *Once Upon a Time in America* conveys the familiar rise-and-fall story of an American gangster. The film's narrative keeps doubling back, to Noodles as a very young man and to his long-lost love affair with Deborah, who dreams of becoming an actress.

"The style of my film," Leone says, "is a tribute to all the American movies I saw and fell in love with as a youth. Today, American movies are like TV soap operas, which are taking over everything. [In 1984] They gave five Oscars to a film [*Terms of Endearment*] which in style is not different from 'Dynasty' and 'Dallas.' " Leone feels that his film is the completion of a trilogy about America that began with *Once Upon a Time in the West* and *A Fistful of Dollars*. A gangster film of epic proportions, it is, Leone feels, not at all like another crime epic, *The Godfather*. He says that *Once Upon a Time in America* has altogether different motivations. He feels that it is essentially a story about friendship, and that despite the film's careful reconstruction of historical environments—among them the incredible transformation of South Eighth Street in the Williamsburg section of Brooklyn—it is basically a fairy tale. About his star, Robert De Niro, he told *Sight and Sound:* "De Niro has always been emblematic of realistic or even hyper-realistic cinema, and the way he and I have adapted to our reciprocal needs and personalities is exactly that something new which made me want all the more to have him in the leading role." There were up to fifty takes for some of the scenes in the film. In one, during which De Niro is awakened by an alarm clock, the actor asked that a different-sounding alarm be used for every take, in order to keep an element of surprise. "I've always wanted to show just one thing in my films," Leone says, "that good goes hand in hand with evil, and that we love Abel only because there is a Cain."

The short version of *Once Upon a Time in America* removes Leone's intricate interweaving of flashbacks that tell the story. Instead, the story is told in a straight, chronological fashion, starting in 1923. A young, dark-haired girl, Deborah, dances alone to a phonograph record in the back room of a Lower East Side tavern. Through a crack in the wall a young boy, Noodles, watches in awe. When the dance is over, the young girl slips out of her dress. It is a vision that young Noodles Aaronson will carry with him the rest of his life.

De Niro's Noodles is perhaps as much lost in the sweeping violence and bloodletting that so character-ize *Once Upon a Time in America,* as the film is lost in the character's ambiguities. Presented at first as a slightly anarchic romantic hero who is humane and self-doubting, he later becomes ferocious, in two rape scenes: the first when he rapes gun moll Carol (Tuesday Weld) and the second when he violently rapes the lost love of his life, Deborah (Elizabeth McGovern), in the back of a limousine. Noodles' sexual hostility is never explained in the movie. Nevertheless, the film's pica-resque jaunt through what appears to be a kind of sor-did macho-romanticism sees De Niro, as always, in a commanding role.

Warner Brothers released the short version of *Once Upon a Time in America* following a series of disastrous previews of Leone's uncut version in Boston, New York, and Los Angeles, where audiences laughed at important moments in the film. The cut version opened in 800 theaters around the country in the spring of 1984. The controversy over both versions spread throughout the world in movie theaters, corpo-rate boardrooms, and the international press. On one side, of course, was Sergio Leone, who feared that an American film company had butchered his ten-year dream, his masterwork. On the other side was film ex-ecutive Alan Ladd, Jr., who admitted that he preferred Leone's long version but felt that he could not release it. Test audiences just were not buying it; and following the disappointing box-office takes of the Ladd Film Company's highly touted *The Right Stuff* (as well as other Warner Brothers releases), the film company was not exactly on a roll. While the rest of the world was able to see Leone's long version, North America was offered the truncated version.

"By not participating in their editing of my film, I remain clean," Leone said. "Because my film is about memory, when they take away flashbacks, it is no longer my film. It can only be a mediocre film about Borsalino hats and guns." In addition to restructuring the film's narrative, the short version also trimmed a number of scenes of De Niro's gang as boys. Also cut back were the roles of Carol and Deborah, who were both to have been seen as old women in the film's 1968 finale. In the longer version, Deborah seems not to have aged at all, which drew laughs of disbelief at one preview. To no one's surprise, however, Robert De Niro was perfectly credible as an old man.

In its short, superedited version, *Once Upon a Time in America* was totally conventional in structure; those events that remained, happened in a linear, chronological fashion. The result was a beautifully photographed and deliciously scored epic that rendered most of the film nearly bloodless. Finally in October 1984, *Once Upon a Time in America* was shown at the New York Film Festival and began an exclusive theatrical run. The version shown was Leone's full version, minus one-and-one-half minutes to meet the requirements of an R rating. This marked the first U.S. exhibition of the director's version, other than the film's prerelease market research screenings.

The uncut version of *Once Upon a Time in America* provides an elegiac dreamscape for the filmgoer.

Leone's world—seen through the eyes of Noodles Aaronson—is a compelling, intoxicating journey through time and the random recollections of lost youth, violated innocence, betrayal, and violently spent lives. On its surface, it is the social history of a small group of gangsters who started out as punks and petty thieves, and whose lives—save for two, Noodles' and Max's—end in carnage. Scratch the surface a little deeper and *Once Upon a Time in America* is the tale—similar in some ways to *1900*—of two men whose lives are bonded together by a mysterious code that neither the women nor the other men in their lives can decipher. Noodles and Max, like Alfredo and Olmo in Bertolucci's film are indeed opposite sides of the same coin. Yet, ultimately, they are divided by the shadow of Max's betrayal.

James Woods, Tuesday Weld, Elizabeth McGovern, Larry Rapp, Joe Pesci, Danny Aiello, and William Forsythe all provide finely tuned character performances. Sadly, one of De Niro's costars in the film, James Hayden, never lived to see the completed film. He died of a heroin overdose after the filming finished.

With *Once Upon a Time in America*, Robert De Niro once again filled the screen with the presence of a street hoodlum. His Noodles Aaronson was the portrait of a young upstart who was always taking orders, holding the bag for a shadowy authority figure. As a young punk, Noodles and company took orders from older, more established criminals. His one courageous act—stabbing a gunman who killed a young comrade—sent him to jail as a boy, but he grew up with no desire to further his life in crime. Yet he was still considered a member of the old gang. Unable to extricate himself from the criminal class and the wealth it bestowed on him, he went along with the status quo, until he finally could not live by the rules Max enforced. His small betrayal resulted in his holding the bag again—for over thirty years. By the end of his life, with his denial of Max, he was finally free, absolved from his overwhelming burden of fear and guilt.

XIV

Bobby and Meryl

"When something happens like two people falling in love, it's as destructive a force as it is creative. I think you have to see that good things are destroyed while other things are created. That's the nature of a passion like this."

So says Michael Cristofer, actor, playwright, and the writer of *Falling in Love*, the 1984 film that pooled the talents of acting superstars Robert De Niro and Meryl Streep with director Ulu Grosbard. Streep and De Niro had not appeared together on film since *The Deer Hunter*, a film for which they both received Academy Award nominations. The pairing of these stars generated a tremendous amount of excitement and also fulfilled their wishes. Ever since *The Deer Hunter*, De Niro says, "I was always thinking of something I could do with Meryl—a play, a movie, anything. . . . We had a reading and began to see possibilities in it. Then

Ulu Grosbard seemed like the right director. . . . Meryl and I had a wonderful time. I'd love to do a straight comedy with her one day."

Falling in Love opens with the hustle and bustle of a workday in full swing as Manhattan-bound commuters ride the Metro-North into New York City from Westchester County. Among the Christmas-time crowd are Frank Raftis (Robert De Niro) and Molly Gilmore (Meryl Streep). She is a graphic artist en route to the city to visit her ailing father, and he is a construction supervisor, consigned to the use of mass transportation until his car is out of the shop. They are both, for the moment, happily married.

Their train reaches its destination, Grand Central Station, Manhattan's beehive of activity, and they each go their separate ways, Frank to his construction site, Molly to her father. By day's end, last-minute Christmas shopping sees Frank at Saks Fifth Avenue asking the advice of a world-weary saleswoman on what color blouse he should buy his wife, Ann (Jane Kaczmarek), or being chastised for eating a hot dog in a crowded elevator: "You shouldn't be eating here," says an irate woman passenger. "People have clothes on." It is at Rizzoli's Bookstore where Molly and Frank meet momentarily, after purchasing gifts for their respective spouses. Both overburdened with gifts, they collide at the door on their way out, exchange a few laughs and self-conscious chuckles, then head their separate ways. Each takes a second to look back at the other, across the din and crowd of Fifth Avenue holiday shoppers. They disappear into the crowd.

If Robert De Niro and Meryl Streep were the stars of *Falling in Love*, then New York City played a respectable supporting role. The winter wonderland of

Manhattan, lusciously photographed by British cinematographer Peter Suschitzky, provided a fairy tale-like ambience for the love that blossomed between Frank and Molly. Cast and crew spent days shooting around Fifth Avenue and Fifty-seventh Street in the spring of 1984. Included among the Fifth Avenue locations were Saks Fifth Avenue, St. Patrick's Cathedral, Trump Tower, and, of course, Rizzoli's. The historical bookstore stayed open for business during the few days that De Niro and company filmed there, as the store's L-shaped structure permitted one part to be closed for filming, while the other was open for customers.

Additionally, spring filming saw Saks Fifth Avenue transformed—all of the store's Christmas decorations were put up for the holiday shopping scenes. Cast, crew, and extras "completely took over the store from its closing on Friday night to its opening on Saturday morning," an insider on the set said. "By the time the store was ready to open on Saturday, the Christmas decorations had once again vanished from sight."

Grand Central Station, usually a hotbed of activity, was the company's second home for weeks. Filming was permitted only in seven-hour sessions, and only between rush hours. Masses of extras were seen pouring through the station at such times as 2:00 P.M. and 2:00 A.M., to simulate morning or evening commuter rush hours. At one point, the usually reticent De Niro invited a photographer to see his trailer, which he used on location. "I'm having a good time shooting this movie," De Niro told the photographer, while happily signing autographs. "Do something cute," the photographer said. At which point, De Niro smiled, rather sheepishly saying, "Gee, I don't know what to do. Actually, this is as cute as I get."

He gets cuter. Months pass before Frank and Molly meet again, and when they do meet, it is again on a New York City-bound train. Their tentative, nervous interplay on the train clearly suggests more than just a passing interest between them, yet their respective spouses loom, unseen, in the backs of their minds. The two seem to dance, guiltily, unavoidably toward each other, and the scene vividly recollects a similar scene that the two actors played out in *The Deer Hunter:* a mild flirtation, perhaps unconscious, with an attendant chorus of "uh-huhs," "yeahs," "okays," and "sures," a flirtation that draws together two people who are meant for each other. Their moments on the train, their nervous flashes of recognition are humorously acknowledged and validated: "Do you work in the city?" Frank asks Molly. "No," she says, "I'm married."

And the ball is rolling. At the construction site and over lunch, Frank tells his friend Ed (Harvey Keitel) about his encounter with Molly. Ed is all ears and is supportive. He is also divorcing his wife. Back at her job, Molly endures a cross-examination from her girlfriend Isabelle (Dianne Wiest). She projects a neurotic, vaguely promiscuous "go for it" to Molly. Molly, exasperated with her friend's inability to perceive and empathize with her confusion over her mounting interest in Frank, dismisses Isabelle's shallow, skeptical advice. "All you think about is sex," Molly says. "I do my best," Isabelle replies. Exhausted, Molly tells her, "I like being with him."

Molly and Frank agree to meet at Grand Central Station later that day for their rush-hour trips home to husband and family. And over coffee and conversation, and what one critic called "sweet clumsiness," the pair succumbs "to an inarticulate need" for one another.

"They are charming statistics that have collided in the random ricochets of modern life," *Newsweek* wrote. Whatever they are, they are full of it at Grand Central Station. Both have no reasons to be unhappy with their respective spouses: Frank's wife is a gem, as a wife, and as a mother to their two sons, and Molly's husband Brian (David Clennon), a doctor, seems sensitive and caring. Yet, Frank and Molly are propelled, earnestly, toward each other.

Soon an afternoon tryst is arranged; the two meet at Rizzoli's before embarking downtown to Greenwich Village's Bank Street, to the apartment Frank has borrowed for the afternoon. Cozily ensconced, the two begin kissing passionately, but, ultimately, do not make love. Molly cannot see it through, and the two finally just sit on the bed, fully clothed, their attempt at infidelity thwarted by conscience.

"It's very sweet to know what's inside people's hearts, instead of what's underneath their clothes, don't you think?" Meryl Streep has said. Indeed, throughout *Falling in Love,* Frank and Molly never do succeed in actually *making* love. "That's the nice thing about it, the not-consummating-it part of it," De Niro recalled. "That's the whole point. Sex in a movie, isn't that the easy thing to do?"

For his role in *Falling in Love,* De Niro recalls, "I did some research on being a construction foreman. But that didn't make my role any easier. I mean, he's not me." Meryl Streep has said that the two of them spent many hours together, over croissants and coffee, in her SoHo loft, going over the Michael Cristofer script. "We wanted something real, something awkward and crumpled," Miss Street has said. "He's incapable of making a fake move. So when there was something wrong with the writing, he just couldn't do it," she recalls. "Then everyone would realize that the scene was wrong and we'd fix it. He's infallible, like a compass. You're never adrift." And as for Meryl Streep? She is a "pure actress," De Niro says, who has "many more colors than people have seen. She's a great comedienne." In fact, De Niro had wanted Streep to play Masha in *The King of Comedy,* but the actress had other commitments. Also, De Niro says of his co-star, "She's in my opinion very beautiful and has a lot of elegance about her. Usually, a woman in that situation tends to be . . . more concerned about . . . how she appears because the beauty sort of gets in the way. Meryl sort of goes against that . . . that's why she's terrific. The old movie stars of the thirties—some of them had more chutzpah, more something other than just being pretty and looked at. That's what Meryl has. She's really an actress."

De Niro says he saw *Falling in Love* "as something to do and I thought I could concentrate on things other than what I usually concentrate on—things like makeup or whatever. But it only appeared to be easier. You always have to worry, you always have to concentrate—it's just more deceptive when you work on the surface."

Director Ulu Grosbard was thrilled with the sublime chemistry that his two stars brought to the film. "They have this genuine, astonishing chemistry together on the screen. If that hadn't been there I wouldn't have touched [the script]." Grosbard has also commented on their other attributes: "You have to remember also that they're both *very* intelligent people. Their intuition, their sense of people, is enormous. She has a very quick mind. De Niro is not as articulate—an example that intelligence and verbal facility don't go hand in hand." There's a purity that De Niro brings to his work, Grosbard says. "He's like a truly fine writer, going take after take, polishing, refining, going for the essence, for the zen stroke, so to speak."

Falling in Love, Grosbard says, "shows a side of Bobby he's never shown—tender, open, understanding, and humorous. It's a lot easier to play an angry scene—but the subtlety of this part was very much harder."

One side of De Niro that was readily shown to all on the set of *Falling in Love* was his exactitude in approaching his role. Michael Cristofer—the Pulitzer Prize and Tony Award winner for his play *The Shadow Box*—made his screenwriting debut with *Falling in Love.* He had heard all the stories about De Niro's obsession for authenticity, yet was nevertheless surprised that the actor wanted him to write a whole set of lines that would never be heard in the film—for the scenes of Frank Raftis talking on the phone to his wife, Ann, De Niro asked Cristofer to write her side of the "dialogue." "It was phenomenal," Cristofer recalls. "I'm not telling tales out of school, but I expected he would improvise everything. He turned out to be the most meticulous craftsman I have ever seen work. Whenever there was a phone call with Ann, he would ask that the other conversation be written out. It's exactness to an amazing degree."

An insider on the set of the film reported an additional striving for authenticity: De Niro had a propman make business cards for him with the name Frank Raftis imprinted on them. The cards were not intended for use in the film, but rather, for De Niro to keep in his wallet during shooting and, presumably, at other times.

Frank and Molly, by now in the nerve- and conscience-racking throes of their forbidden love (despite their failed attempt at lovemaking) go their separate ways—for the moment. Shaken by their afternoon encounter on Bank Street, Molly sits for awhile in her car after pulling into her driveway. Her husband comes out of the house with bad news. The hospital called to say that her father has died. A couple of days later, at the funeral, her sobs of grief over the death of her father completely overtake her. Her husband leads her away from the funeral to their car, but she is inconsolable, frantically trying to remove his grasp from her shoulders—her breakdown, unbeknownst to her husband, has less to do with the death of her father than it does with her relationship with Frank. She is physically manifesting the turbulent changes and contradictory feelings brought about by her shift in affections. From the burden of all this, and the weight of the guilt she feels, she collapses. He and I are meant for each other, she tells Isabelle while convalescing at home. But we will never be together.

Frank, who by this time has been offered a lucrative position in Houston by his construction company, is confronted by his wife soon before they are to move to Texas. He comes home late one night; she is waiting up for him. De Niro's face is sheer gravity as he tries to respond to his wife's query about his moods lately. He explains, haltingly, that he met a woman on the train and that they have been spending time together in the city. As if trying to reassure her of his faithfulness, he tells her that, no, they've never slept together. She sees right through him. Of course he hasn't been physically unfaithful to her. "No," she says, "it's worse than that, isn't it?" She knows that he desperately wants to be unfaithful, that he is no longer in love with her. She slaps him across his face.

Ann goes to Colorado with their sons to visit her mother, to sort things out. Frank stays behind and sees to it that their house is readied for the movers. On his last night before flying out West, he calls Molly. He would like to see her before he leaves. She declines, but after she hangs up the phone she changes her mind and sets out into the rainy night for one last visit. This is the straw that breaks the back of her marriage to Brian. He tries to prevent her from leaving but fails. Unaware that she has changed her mind and is en route to him, Frank calls again, only to get Brian on the phone. He tells Frank to leave his wife alone once and for all. He tells him that she has gone to bed. On her way to see Frank, Molly's car stalls at a railroad crossing and she narrowly escapes being hit by an oncoming train. Frank leaves by cab for the airport. And it would seem that any chance of a reconciliation is gone for good. But in the great tradition of happy endings—and in the tradition of never sending a film audience home depressed—Molly and Frank get a second chance.

Almost a year later, Frank comes back to New York, leaving a failed marriage behind in Texas. It is Christmas time again, and the familiar environs of Fifth Avenue and Fifty-seventh Street draw both Molly and Frank to Rizzoli's Bookstore. They greet each other politely and exchange their lives' recent stories—Molly not letting on to Frank that her marriage, too, has failed. Their encounter is fraught with tension for the viewer because neither one "comes clean" with the other. Instead, they exchange awkward "good-byes" and "Merry Christmases" and go their separate ways. Out on the street, though, Frank acts on his emotions after looking back at Molly, who is fast disappearing into the crowd toward Grand Central Station. He chases after her. In the holiday din of a Metro-North railroad car they finally glimpse each other across a sea of heads. They move toward each other, jostled along the way by the train's vast expanse of passengers. They embrace.

Falling in Love reminded many filmgoers of the 1946 film *Brief Encounter,* with Celia Johnson and Trevor Howard. Indeed, *Falling in Love* seemed to play homage to the London-set story in which two people who meet on a train station platform fall helplessly— but quite hopelessly—in love. Their affair is never consummated, and the two—she a housewife, he a doctor —ultimately go their separate ways for good. *Falling in Love*'s connection to *Brief Encounter,* Ulu Grosbard says, ". . . Occurred to me when I read the script, even before I started to make the film. I examined the problem very carefully, because you take your life in your hands when you make a movie reminiscent of a classic like that. But I was determined to give *Falling in Love* its own integrity . . . it's very unusual material for me, a bit more romantic than my usual taste. My instinct was to try and anchor the story in a measured reality, not to make it gushy."

Given the moral climate of 1946, a "happy ending" for an almost-adulterous couple would have raised eyebrows. But not in 1984. "The fabric of marriage is far more fragile today," Grosbard says. "The possibility of an affair like this occurring is much truer, much more believable that it would have been forty years ago." And as for *Falling in Love*'s coda, with its seemingly improbable reunion of Frank and Molly, Grosbard says, "You go for the possible, not the probable. It comes from Hawthorne—I have to paraphrase. Something like: As long as you're faithful to the truths of the human heart the writer has 'a fair right'—I'm sure of those words—to create his own circumstance."

The circumstances of *Falling in Love* provided unprecedented new territory for Robert De Niro—rather placid territory, given the physical, emotional extremes of his earlier films. "I was tired," De Niro says. "This script came along. It was a nice story, set here in New York." As usual, the "risk" of trying something new was no obstacle to the actor whose career has seen him take many risks indeed. "I don't always have to do high-risk parts. I thought it was something different than I've done before, and for that reason alone it was a good reason to do it."

XV

Through a Glass Darkly?

It is very likely that Robert De Niro's achievement may lie in the fact that there appears to be no one else capable of rendering the characters he has played. His disturbed portraits have no equals in cinema. They are, in themselves, paradigms. Perhaps what sets him apart from other actors is his ability to tune his instrument finely to within a hair's breadth of his own flesh, or, more clearly, his ability to render characters that seem to spring readily from his own self. If the filmgoer is a little frightened by what Robert De Niro becomes on the screen, it is not at all surprising. De Niro plays his roles so close to the self that one's first impulse is to worry for De Niro's well-being, as when Jake La Motta takes a nasty, noisy crunch to the face. You don't say to yourself, "What a great actor," you say "Ouch! That hurt!" It's a little scary.

In worrying for De Niro's well-being, in seeing the

risks he so freely takes with himself and his body, you arrive at the implication that not only does he know what he's doing to himself, what he's subjecting himself to, but that he must enjoy it. You're tempted to say "It's not acting." It's certainly not fantasy. It's almost perverse. Indeed, there are some who would say that it is *definitely* perverse. Whatever it is, it is unequaled.

His achievements have, up to this point, been the shared glory of a great army of devotees, somewhat larger than a cult following. It's better this way, for it keeps his integrity very much intact. There are other actors of his generation whose integrity has gone the way of all overexposed flesh, who have become too-readily-available commodities, who are, in short, no longer interesting.

But none of this seems to pinpoint what it *is* that brings it all together in Robert De Niro. It is barely possible to draw comparisons, but when they are drawn, the word Brando is most often spoken. Probably no one since Marlon Brando has evinced such a stunning capacity to expose the visceral, the secret self the way De Niro does. It makes no difference that so many of his roles have been unappealing characters, whom you might not want to meet on *any* street. De Niro is graced with one further, incontrovertible blessing: he cannot be imitated. The Brando trademark is best characterized by the often imitated "I coulda been a contender" or by the primal "Stellaaaaa" of Stanley Kowalski. There is not, however, a generation of actors running around like Travis Bickle saying, "I want to be a person like other people" or like Rupert Pupkin saying, in his offbeat stand-up comedy collage, "Better to be a king for a night than a schmuck for a lifetime."

Brando tapped the ore of a restive collective consciousness, strip-mined it, and gave it a gravelly voice —a voice that to this day can be said to ring true. It's archetypal. De Niro has said something shockingly, uncomfortably different. He has created a collection of shrewd, intelligent, and lonely demons with a propensity for outrageous acts and, quite often, a sense for humor. They are all unlike anyone you have ever encountered or are likely to encounter. They are uniquely his now, and Travis Bickle's "You talkin' to me . . .?" off-the-wall speech is probably De Niro's only piece of dialogue that has slipped into the mainstream of everyday usage. De Niro stands absolutely alone in what he does with his craft. What follows is a brief summary.

Jon Rubin of *Greetings* and *Hi, Mom!* shifts from the relatively mod stance of a late sixties left-leaning hipster to a Vietnam vet, a racist cop with a message, and finally to a demolitions expert, blowing up housing projects. A hodgepodge of identities, he is the seed for the much later personality/identity breakdown of *Taxi Driver*'s Travis. He is at once sweet-seeming and murderously close to the edge. You don't know where he stands. You don't trust him.

With *Bloody Mama,* De Niro's momentary Lloyd Barker is probably the only memorable abberation in the film. It is perhaps treason to admit this, but Lloyd Barker is arguably more terrifying in his mindless heroin craze and frothing, rabid presence, than Johnny Boy is in *Mean Streets.* Johnny Boy is a self-contained crackpot. He seems like Lloyd Barker without the drugs. He's an organic nut, he's au natural. Lloyd Barker is a frightful, unspeakable blend of the needle and family inbreeding.

In *Bang the Drum Slowly,* De Niro flirts with the idea of a sympathetic character, or at least, an almost sympathetic character. For, as poignant as Bruce Pearson's dilemma is, it is his *dilemma,* not Bruce himself, that caused tears to well up in moviegoer's eyes. De Niro's skill in the film is in rendering a generally unlikable character in such a way that, despite his irritating flaws of personality, the filmgoer responds to him with a measure of humanity. If Bruce Pearson were not dying of Hodgkin's disease, he would be written off as a boor.

With *Mean Streets* and De Niro's organically nutty Johnny Boy, the sound barrier was cracked: De Niro's name was shouted everywhere, and for apparent reasons he became closely associated with that type of role. But that type of role ended there, in 1973. From that point on, a sort of brainlessness vanished. Henceforth, De Niro's characters, no matter how twisted, tortured, or ill at ease, would have their own inimitable inner logic. They would march to their own drums, they would have a method to their madness.

As the young Vito, De Niro convinced the world of at least two things: by putting the lid on his manic energy he could come up looking stunningly attractive and evince tremendous grace, style, and power (with fewer than ten lines of dialogue); and he could harness the mannerisms and cool ambitiousness that won Marlon Brando an Oscar and in so doing fetch one for himself. Nothing like that had ever been done before. In paying homage to the master of Method he established himself as the Method's new master.

Taxi Driver, of course, is De Niro's most talked-about film, the film that is most closely associated with him. It is also the film that did best at the box office. It firmly established the De Niro/Scorsese team as a force to be reckoned with, and it established De Niro as the perfect embodiment of all that, justifiably or not, was wrong with American urban society. Travis Bickle put a stamp of credibility on urban vigilantism, but he in no way put an end to the possibility of further De Niro growth, or an end to the personalities the actor could pull out of all those hats that he used to wear on Fourteenth Street.

1900 and *The Last Tycoon* didn't catapult him to higher grounds, nor, more importantly, did they diminish his standing. Bertolucci's epic can be said to have equalized De Niro amidst a handful of respectable peers. With *The Last Tycoon,* the curious and enigmatic Monroe Stahr bore an inscrutable weight. It marked, perhaps, the first time that De Niro's face was given plenty of opportunities to register intense private burdens. Appropriately, it was Elia Kazan, one of the Method's oldest living teachers, who was behind the camera.

De Niro became a real musician in *New York, New York.* In his incredible portrayal of saxophonist and of Liza Minnelli's lover, he managed to dismantle any preconceived notions that anybody seeing him act for the first time might have had. It was more than just an offbeat choice for De Niro; it seemed to come out of the blue. Here, surely, was an actor who was in it only to see all of his dreams come true. It was as if De Niro was fulfilling a promise he had made to himself as a kid, to be anything and everything he wanted to be when he grew up. By 1977, he had a technique that no one could put a handle on, that no one could imitate and say, "Okay, now I'm doing De Niro."

If Vito Corleone had been born five or six decades later, he would have been a Clairton, Pennsylvania, steelworker named Michael Vronsky. Surely Vronsky inherited the grace and strength of Corleone, and the silent, stoic, family-loving good-will of such an avuncular hero. With Southeast Asia falling down around him and his friends crushed beyond repair in the war-torn debris, Vronsky emerges a slightly skewed saint. He is a questionable hero, and an awkward lover to Meryl Streep when he comes home. His conscience tells him that his medals of honor are only memories of a horror from which he just barely escaped. De Niro's Vronsky could easily have been Travis Bickle as a Green Beret in Vietnam, so easily does he manage to keep the filmgoer poised between respect for what he's been through and fear for how and when his nightmares will erupt. You want to regard him as a hero but you wouldn't want to place money on him.

Nor would you necessarily want to place any money on the suggested virtues of De Niro's Jake La Motta. Is De Niro Jake, or is Jake De Niro? If *Raging Bull* was a test for De Niro's physical endurance far beyond anything he had ever done, so it was a test for the De Niro faithful. It clearly demonstrated that De Niro was as much interested in exploring all the possible permutations of body as he was in demonstrating all the permutations the mind could endure. There was no limit to what he would go through. He didn't care that filmgoers saw him as half an ounce of humanity and 220 pounds of sin.

By 1982, the stops were pulled out. You would have thought that De Niro had done it all—but, now, a priest, a monsignor? *True Confessions* was less of De Niro the actor than of De Niro the face. Ulu Grosbard covered every inch of it—still slightly plump from *Raging Bull*—not missing any of its features, from the mole on the upper right cheek to its more subtle manifesta-

tions, such as guilt, an awkwardly empty (for a monsignor) expression of piousness, ambition, indiscretion.
Put two actors of great talent and integrity together
and it doesn't matter what the box-office printout reads.
There is no substitute for quality acting and the stirring
truths that divide two rival brothers. And De Niro's
face registers sensitivity truthfully.

Time for something light. As Rupert Pupkin, he
played Rupert Pupkin playing Bob Hope, Jerry Lewis,
Buddy Hackett—all brilliantly badly. De Niro's Pupkin
was a ridiculously winning combination of off-the-wall
nerd and ingratiating, unctuous sleaze. To see De Niro
sidle up to the mike, to hear him reel off a battery of
borscht-belt boffo one-liners, is worth the price of admission. Up until now, straight comedy was the missing
component in his body of work. In this pairing with
Jerry Lewis, the laughs were italicized by the film's
dark, brooding commentary on fame; and Rupert Pupkin, like Bruce Pearson, was the oddball loner whom
filmgoers loved to hate—or hated to love.

Sergio Leone also insisted on a romance with De
Niro's face. *Once Upon a Time in America* used it as its
centerpiece in the epic treatment of Noodles Aaronson's memories. Already a classic in its own right, the
film seems to comment on and make use of all of De
Niro's personae. His face is a holy presence throughout
the film. It is the first one you see in the peace of a
narcotic state and the one you see, equally riveting, in
its old age, registering an innocence long ago lost. At
forty-two, De Niro has shown the world what to expect
when he's sixty-two.

With *Falling in Love,* De Niro made a rather perverse choice of playing as close to a matinee idol as he
probably ever will: an upper-middle-class husband hav-

ing an unconsummated affair with an equally upper-middle-class married woman. He finally did what everyone was wondering if he could do—he played somebody *normal*. And with that, he confirmed that, to date, he is absolutely unpredictable. Who is like Robert De Niro, which actor is it? There is only one answer to that question: There are no contenders.

Perhaps the one thing that De Niro's long list of personality types hasn't done is invite the viewer in. While each of De Niro's gems has an amazing inner compass that guides him to his destiny, filmgoers are hard put to enter—to feel welcome—into the hearts of the characters De Niro has assembled. While there is no doubt that Bickle and family follow and feel their own heartbeats, it can be said that filmgoers, while amazed at what the actor becomes on the screen, quite often do not feel inclined to experience what a Michael Vronsky experiences inside or what a Travis Bickle experiences. In this way, the frustrated energies of the actor's characters are quite often unsympathetically acknowledged. De Niro's people have a mesmerizing look-but-don't-touch air about them. They bear a stamp of unapproachability, carry the all-familiar baggage of alienated, self-absorbed modern living. De Niro's people aren't necessarily rebels without causes, or, for that matter, rebels with causes. They simply see no point of entry into society, no avenues of approach into the mainstream. They're scared by this. To create and sustain lives for themselves, they invent moral codes, operate in closed sets. They decorate their vacuums. They are sealed off from the world at large, and the world at large is sealed off from them. Each side looks at the other, through a glass darkly.

De Niro's achievement has been to create a world of frantic, graceful beings tuned to perfect pitch—but only to themselves. What many filmgoers are waiting for is a chance to connect with them in a heartfelt way on some shared middle ground. With De Niro's most recent films in mind, it is quite possible that this will occur.

XVI

Diahnne Abbott

Probably no marriage in Tinsel Town has caused as much head turning as that of Robert De Niro and Diahnne Abbott. They were married in 1976, amid a bevy of show-business friends. Although there were press reports in 1978 telling of a separation, there is no way of knowing whether the separation is a legal one or just a case of two artists doing their own respective things.

Abbott is a beautiful black actress who has appeared in a number of films, most recently in John Cassavetes' *Lovestreams* as a sultry, sweet-voiced nightclub singer. She appeared in a torrid, silent love scene in *Welcome to L.A.*, which Robert Altman produced in 1977, and has appeared in three films that starred Robert De Niro: *Taxi Driver, New York, New York,* and *The King of Comedy.* In *Taxi Driver,* she plays an usherette at the refreshment counter in one of the porno theaters Travis Bickle frequents. She looks on, half-amused, half-detached as Travis makes up his mind about what kind of refreshments he wants to buy. It's a brief, short appearance for the actress: she plays off Travis' manic sensibility like a cool earth-mother.

In *New York, New York*, she appears three-quarters of the way through the film. She sings "Honeysuckle Rose" at a Harlem nightclub, with the dark sensuous presence of a Gauguin painting come to life. It is one of the film's memorable moments. "I was standing up there, feeling really pleased about the way I looked," she recalls. "Suddenly the spots went on and I thought 'What on earth am I doing here?' I felt a terrible sense of panic. I was six years old again, but instead of primping in front of mother's vanity, I was acting in front of a real movie crew. I thought, 'My God, this is it.' "

Diahnne Abbott has come a long way from her waitress days in New York City, the days of hanging out in Washington Square Park, the days of discouragement in her career. "It's hard enough for a woman to act nowadays, but a black woman has an even harder time. It's as if the people with power are only interested in actors who make up 'The Big Dozen.' " Anyone else is considered worthless. Of course, the so-called Big Dozen includes her husband, Robert De Niro. "Being married to a star can have good and bad results," she says. "I can meet more people. But often, producers don't think of me when they're casting. They think of me only as the wife of a star." Her struggle is a solitary one, she says, regardless of whom she is married to. "I'm doing this all by myself, just as if I were a single woman or married to someone who works for the sanitation department. My husband has been through it all and I know he probably feels for me. But he's also a source of inspiration to me." When she met De Niro, he was a struggling actor living in Greenwich Village. "I thought he was marvelous," she says, "but I never expected him to be a star." She speaks of De Niro's obsession with the roles he plays. Her husband, she says, gets "so wrapped up in his character that you don't know him." His commitment to his work and family gives her strength: "Now I think it's possible to do good work, be creative, keep your integrity and still get to be famous in America."

Rearing a family (she has a daughter, Drina, by a previous marriage and a son, Raphael, by De Niro) *and* pursuing a professional acting and singing career is a task that not many women would find enviable, but Abbott manages well, it would seem. "I grew up hearing all the time that if a woman was a real woman, and had a man's love and his children, then she couldn't have a career too. It was something that I absolutely believed. Well, I want to prove to myself that a woman can do it."

One Manhattan restaurateur remembers the days when Diahnne Abbott, not yet well known, would create a stir merely by walking across a street. "She was an exceptional beauty," he recalls. "Her stunning good looks created a stir all along Tenth Street. One night, years later, someone phoned in a reservation at the restaurant; 'semi-celebrity' status, they said. And who should walk in, with an entourage, but Diahnne Abbott. Looking just gorgeous, really breathtaking. She was becoming known by then—and she knew it. She was very conscious of the heads that turned when she made her entrance. One of my waiters almost dropped a tray of hors d'oeuvres."

Abbott believes that most female roles are projections of male fantasies that have really very little to do with the reality of being a woman. "With all of the great actresses in New York and California, when a producer casts a role, he uses a fashion model. I don't understand that. . . . You know, when I was trying to model in the early sixties, I used to meet women who were obsessed with meeting men and money. I never felt that way. I absolutely, positively believed in love. It didn't pay the bills, but I was romantic and I still am. Now, I'd like to do a very good love story. One that doesn't have a happy ending. Most love stories don't have happy endings."

In *The King of Comedy*, she plays Rupert Pupkin's girlfriend, and in it their love story does not have a happy ending. As his former high-school sweetheart, she patiently goes along with his madcap plans to ingratiate himself into the life of comedian Jerry Langford. Lonely and working as a barmaid, she evinces a grand solitude, a life bereft of dreams, a life of missed chances.

The living arrangement that De Niro and Abbott have worked out is a curious one, although it seems to work for them. They reportedly maintain separate residences, pursue other romances, and spend time together when the mood is right. One friend is quoted as saying, "They break up and then they are together. It's been that way for years. . . . They just go their own way and see each other when they feel like it." De Niro chooses to spend the majority of his time in New York City, and Abbott lives in Beverly Hills. Even when filming *Raging Bull* in Los Angeles, right near his wife, De Niro stayed by himself. "De Niro stayed in a hotel by himself throughout the filming," said a friend of the two, "and while Robert was out there, I would usually see Diahnne going to parties alone without him." Says Abbott on the couple's "not-so-unusual" arrangement: "Robert and I have our own views on life—and they don't particularly mean we have to be together all the time."

XVII

The Hero
Behind the
Masks

There seems very little that Robert De Niro hasn't done as an actor. From bicyclist to baseball catcher, from Don to taxi driver, from tycoon to sax player, from bloated boxer to commuting lover, it's all there. You don't need press blurbs to tell you, you don't need rave reviews to show you what's plain to see on the silver screen. Reams have been written about him, and will continue to be written, no doubt. There will perhaps be more books. And, thankfully, there will be more films.

The man of a hundred faces is known by millions who have seen his many-colored beasts and beauties over the past sixteen years. Yet one face eludes them all —the face of the hero behind the mask. It's hard to believe he's human after all, but most likely he is. He also puts in long days on the job. He's a husband, a loving patriarch, and a son.

There's been much talk of his reclusiveness, of

privacy, of Greta Garbo affectations. Most of it is explainable; some of it isn't. Yet he'll be the first one to tell you that human nature at its best or worst isn't always explainable. He knows, because Travis Bickle knows, because Michael Vronsky knows. Everyone knows. To start with, there's the small matter of his job, his work. "I'm just not 'on' all the time," he has said. "I think you find an awful lot of people in my profession who are basically shy and introverted by nature, and their extrovert qualities—in my case, I know—are limited to their work." When De Niro does a character like Travis Bickle, he does more than spend time at the Bronx Zoo looking at caged animals. "When I do a character like Michael Vronsky, the steelworker in *The Deer Hunter*, I try to make him appear as real as if I'd known him all my life." Therefore, he says, ". . . It's not too easy for me to flip back out of character and come off camera." Hence De Niro's angry moodiness on the set of *Taxi Driver*, his cantankerous stance on the set of *Raging Bull*, and his beaming approachability on the set of *Falling in Love*. "Actually, I have to keep my energies up and anything that disturbs that is a negative force to me. . . . I'm interested in what motivates a character I'm playing and I really don't like to be distracted when I'm working on these things. So maybe I sublimate my own personality in order to get the totality of the role."

Producer Michael Phillips corroborates De Niro's intractability on this score, saying that "Bobby is quiet anyway. But when he's working he has to have the luxury of self-involvement in order to turn in the kind of performance he does."

If there is anything De Niro waxes eloquent

about, it is his acting. And rightfully so, for he represents the state of the art. "Acting isn't really respected enough as an art," he says. "Your body is an instrument, and you have to learn how to play an instrument." Naturally. De Niro brings that metaphor to life in *New York, New York;* he's such a pro that even today he can be heard playing "Misty" on his own tenor saxophone. And he talks about Brando: "Early Brando seemed to romanticize, but it's really the poetry of his whole being—I don't know about my poetry, but you just look at Brando and you're interested. He has a sense of truth in all his instincts." In order to get to that sense of truth, De Niro says, "It is important not to indicate. People don't indicate when they tell you about their traumas, they tell it pretty much flat out. People don't try to show you their feelings, they try to hide them. It is important to keep it fresh and simple."

Once, Michael Moriarty, who co-starred with De Niro in *Bang the Drum Slowly,* was watching the actor shoot a scene at the Bellmore Cafeteria for *Taxi Driver.* A production assistant offered to take Moriarty over to De Niro. "No, don't bother," Moriarty said. "I don't know that guy at all. I knew Bruce Pearson. I don't know Travis Bickle or Bob De Niro."

As a child, it seems that De Niro was virtually gifted with a sort of independence rarely given children. He was free to ramble as he chose, and, choosing survival first, he was equipped to ramble further than most. The lower Manhattan finishing school—Hester Street, Kenmare Street—is a tough one to survive in, and it is there, on those streets, where the child became the youth. "Bobby Milk" ran with a gang (". . . Those guys are still around . . ."), but he was also a loner, observing all of life, soaking it all in. But of that lower Manhattan street life, all the colors of the "types" he knew and did not know were not wasted on "Bobby Milk." They made lasting impressions, comprising an internalized gallery whose subjects could only be displayed via acting. De Niro was lucky, he says, because his parents "never bothered me about wanting to be an actor." He took his first acting lessons at The New School at the age of ten.

He worked long and hard in the years that followed. "I got my first jobs without an agent. Sent out my résumés and pictures and showed up at auditions. When you're starting out, you really have to do it all by yourself. And you still end up having to do it all by yourself. I don't like people to make decisions for me."

His fascination with "experiencing" what he calls the facts of a character, his unfettered and seemingly unquenchable curiosity coupled with what he has said about acting being a "cheap way to do things you would never do in real life," suggest that he is a man interested in possibilities, possibilities that entail a minimum of risk. Yet he has, on at least one occasion, risked his life to experience the possibility of being a soldier in Vietnam. He has risked his health to experience what it is like to be an overweight, gone-to-seed, former boxing champion. He pushes aside vanity and ego to experience possibilities. What nurtures such an odd desire? What makes such a dedicated man? "I doubt if he knows how good he is," Brando once said.

As heady or sophisticated the household was that nurtured De Niro, it was also a household of two fiercely independent artists who chose not to have any other children. Robert, Jr., lived with his mother from the age of two, after his parents divorced. There seems no doubt that the young Robert was loved by both his parents, that he was not denied opportunities. Yet from the beginning it seemed that the reclusive life of the artist was his calling. His mother abandoned her promising career as an artist to bring Bobby up. Although Italian by name, the young De Niro had more of his mother's Irish in him than anything else and perhaps in that respect was different from the other kids in Little Italy. His father, Robert, Sr., did not have the public recognition in those years that he does now. He travelled widely, was always respected, but was little known. He was teaching at four and five places at once, and "not making any money, a nightmare." Yet he remains a happy, approachable man who seems to make friends easily.

It has been suggested that perhaps the reason Robert, Jr., is not as effervescent as his father is that he felt trapped living with his mother and her boyfriend Manny Farber, a painter and film critic. In those early years, *Redbook* says, Farber was known for his "strong opinions and irascible nature . . . and De Niro, who requires as much courtesy and devotion from his associates as he gives them, may have been relieved when his mother and Farber separated." Apparently, De Niro, Jr., and Farber were reintroduced years later at a Hollywood party. "Do you remember me?" Farber asked the now celebrated actor. "I used to go out with your mother. You have unbelievable eyes. Just like your father. You're much more like your father than your mother." According to people present at the party, De Niro bolted. Then there is the story of the party thrown for him by a Hollywood hostess, following his tour de force performances in *Bang the Drum Slowly* and

Mean Streets. When word got out that De Niro would probably show up at the party, literally hundreds of people were said to have shown up. "I was looking everywhere for him," *Redbook* reports the hostess as saying. "Then somebody came in and said two bums were outside in the bushes. I went out and it was De Niro talking to Al Pacino. He was afraid to come inside."

There are hundreds of such stories, that are as telling of a man who is, by nature, introverted, as they are of the unquenchable thirst that the public has for the lives of celebrities. It is perhaps a commonplace that many people feel their own lives would be immeasurably enriched by knowing about the private lives of the rich or the famous. It is perhaps not commonplace enough that such details seldom yield useful information. Artistry alone is its best teacher, and the curious can have much to learn by just watching or hearing the artist speak of his craft. Like a great painter who works behind color and stroke to let a picture speak for itself, or like a virtuoso pianist who loses himself behind the keys to best serve the integrity and truth on a page of music, De Niro serves his craft without a vestige of intrusive personality. "There's nothing more offensive to me than watching an actor act with his ego," he says. "Some of the old movie stars were terrific, but they romanticized. People chase illusions and their illusions are created by movies." De Niro, in his art, gives no illusions. His "shock of becoming" is what separates him from most of his colleagues. "Sometimes I write out a biography to find out what the person would do in other situations, all kinds of situations. It's complicated. You can't know more than the character but as an actor I have to know. All I have to do is know who I am. Does that make any sense?"

Shelley Winters, ever ready to speak on the subject of De Niro, her "Jewish son," says, "Sometimes Bobby gives the impression that he's dumb, that his mind is wiped out because he doesn't say anything. But behind those slit eyes, he's watching everything. . . . I've never seen an actor do the kind of exploration, the minute research that he does for a role. He doesn't act, he *becomes.* He scares me. The things that he does with his body are truly frightening. He can blush or get white as a sheet in a second and he could force his hair to curl on command if he wanted to." Winter remembers a meal shared with Diahnne Abbott and Robert De Niro at a four-star restaurant in Paris at which the waiters seemed arrogant and pretentious. "Bobby can seem very anonymous, but he studies people like a hawk . . . [the waiters] kept telling us where Napoleon sat. I mean, please, let's just get some food . . . but we were being ignored. Then I saw Bobby go through a kind of transformation. He wasn't Bobby anymore. He had decided to play the ugly American. What a performance! He knew that's what they expected."

De Niro says that there is a certain combination of anarchy and discipline in the way he works. "Something that helps me is the physical feeling of the character, the props, the costumes, the way he stands, gestures. I am aware of the physical. It is important. Sometimes it is easier to distinguish a character physically. You make a choice and develop it."

De Niro has been making choices and developing them for a long time. Friends say that all of those choices are part-and-parcel of the baggage he carries with him through life—that he is the sum of the many parts he has played. What privacy he seems to have time for—it seems that he's *always* working—is closely guarded by those friends. One writer, who was interviewing a friend of the actor for an article, found her interview cut short by a phone call—De Niro himself had called his friend and told him not to cooperate. "Now that he's a star," an actor friend said, "he's in an incredible position to help us. Nobody wants to jeopardize that. People are afraid of him now."

The curious are more likely to catch slivers of the man behind the masks by keeping a trained eye on newspaper columns or magazines, where all manner of celebrity tidbits—true and imagined—surface. To what extent reported items are verifiable is left up to the imagination. De Niro has been married to actress Diahnne Abbott since 1976. Their wedding, at New York's Ethical Culture Society, was attended by a large group of show-business colleagues, among them Sam Spiegel, Elia Kazan, John Hancock, Shelley Winters, Julie Bovasso, Joe Papp, Martin Scorsese, Harvey Keitel, and Sally Kirkland. "Everybody there," Paul Schrader recalls, "was somebody who helped Bobby become a different person."

It was reported in 1982 that De Niro became the father of a baby girl, Nina, by Helena Springs, a beautiful black singer/songwriter and former backup vocalist for Bob Dylan. De Niro is said to have deluged Miss Springs with gifts, money, and clothes, and a special trust fund at the time of Nina's birth. *Rolling Stone* reported Miss Springs as denying that the child is De Niro's, but added that she felt "betrayed" that her liaison with De Niro became known to the public.

Friends and colleagues of the actor are tight-lipped when approached to speak on the subject of De Niro himself. Loyalty runs deep in the De Niro circles. Perhaps De Niro himself sums it up best: "Why do people want to know what I had for breakfast?" he once asked. "After my first movies I gave interviews. Then I thought, what's so important about where I went to school, and hobbies? What does that have to do with acting, with my own head? Nothing." On the subject of interviews he says, "After I give an interview, I spend all of my time explaining to people what I meant—or not explaining." He can be remote on the set. "I don't socialize with the actors or the leading lady. It is better to keep a certain sensitivity, that delicate illusion."

Even close friends of De Niro are accustomed to gatherings at which the actor says little more than hello, thank you, or good-bye. Yet, between the hellos and good-byes there is always food. "De Niro loves to eat," actor Donald Sutherland says, "and he goes at it the same way he does acting—with notebook and everything." *Time* wrote that ". . . the silent De Niro can suddenly wax lyrical on the empyrean pasta of glory of cappelletta con proscuitto." It has been said that when De Niro is the host of a party, it has no center, no focal point. He will say almost nothing to his guests all evening long, but rather, nods his head, grins, and occasionally says something like, "Yeah, guys, hey, hey, hey, guys, hey, that's too much." "It takes years to get to know Bobby," Brian DePalma once said. "For instance, he's very bright, but that intelligence comes like flashes of brilliant light and only after you know him for a long time."

Martin Scorsese, who perhaps knows De Niro best of all and has seen him in all seasons, says, "Bobby is always pictured as being this very reclusive guy with angst and he isn't. A lot of his fooling is done among friends. He's a terrific mime. I'll fly with him and he'll mime terror so the stewardess will get him a drink."

De Niro's life has so much to do with acting that it is difficult to imagine him as having a private life at all. He receives more than a dozen scripts a week and those films he selects provide encompassing psychological adventures that demand months of preparation and refinement and, quite often, extensive travel.

He is a blur of activity, a whirling dervish who finds "home" between films in Los Angeles, New York City, and Long Island. In Manhattan, his Hudson Street digs boast a panoramic view of the city. Its interior is replete with a red oak atrium, entranceway, and flooring, redwood master bedroom with skylight and cedar paneling, and a private gym. A legal controversy involving the construction of a twenty-five-by-eight-foot audiovisual cabinet, which its carpenter was said to have never completed, resulted in De Niro's having to pay not only the $15,000 for the job, but interest and the carpenter's legal expenses as well. "I treated him just like another customer," the carpenter said, "and he found that difficult because he's used to people kissing his butt." De Niro's lawyer responded: "Bob's ego? Nonsense. We felt the carpenter was being greedy, but obviously the court didn't. If Bob was that kind of person, how did he and the carpenter get along working together for two years? I've never seen Bob lose his temper . . . he is pleasant, considerate, thoughtful."

Upcoming projects include a cameo in Terry Gilliam's upcoming movie, *Brazil* and, at the time of this writing, there is talk of a biographical film on the life of George Gershwin, to be directed by De Niro's longtime collaborator, Martin Scorsese. One can almost imagine De Niro taking lessons from someone like pianist Bobby

Short. Also reportedly in the works is *Lermontov,* a film
about the life of the Russian romantic poet Mikhail
Yur'evich Lermontov, who was killed in a gun duel in
1841. The film is to be directed by Martin Scorsese,
with a screenplay by Michael Powell, who wrote the
classic *The Red Shoes.*

On rumors of his playing Jesus Christ in another
much-talked-about, pending Scorsese epic, *The Last
Temptation of Christ,* De Niro says, "I don't know. The
role has been done so many times that it's almost like
doing Hamlet. I just don't have any interest. I ran into
Marty in Paris at the end of making *Once Upon a Time
in America.* My head was shaved on top, and my hair
on the sides was colored. I said, 'Come on, do I look like
I can play Christ?' " Certainly, by this time in his career
De Niro disciples could supply a ready answer to that
question.

Thus, flights of the imagination lead one to wonder
just what lies in Robert De Niro's future. He has lived
a ripe, full life, at forty-two, on screen and off. He has
been the toast of the town and of the movie industry,
for more than fifteen years. And he has come a long way
from the status of "Hollywood brat." A long way from
the tenth anniversary party of Francis Ford Coppola's
American Zoetrope Studios—where a handful of
dumpy cheerleaders kicked, a brass band played
"Happy Birthday," and De Niro, along with Wim
Wenders and Dennis Hopper, chanted "We will rule
Hollywood . . ."

It is safe to say that De Niro could "rule Hollywood" if he wanted to, but, more than likely, he would
prefer to rule New York City, specifically, the New
York stage. In interviews he has alluded to his desire to
work on stage again—he's just waiting for the right

script to come along. With whom might he work? Perhaps Martin Scorsese. In fact, before the movie *Raging Bull,* the two had decided to bring the life of Jake La Motta to the stage, in a play entitled *Prizefighter,* with a screen portrayal of La Motta's life planned for later. In all likelihood, it was the offer that De Niro got to play Michael Vronsky in *The Deer Hunter* that saw this project put aside. Chances are that if a Broadway project came along De Niro would be sharing the stage with more than a few of his favorite acting colleagues. It is easy to imagine him under the glare of the stage lights with such stars as Harvey Keitel or with co-star Meryl Streep, who, like De Niro, gained recognition on the stage before entering the film world.

Has he any interest in directing? He has said that he has—and it seems likely that he would be the kind of director actors would love. He would undoubtedly give actors all the support that they need, in a professional way, like a "coach," allowing actors with good instincts the room they need for experimentation. Once asked if he thought director Martin Scorsese, who had small parts in *Taxi Driver* and *King of Comedy,* wanted to be in front of the camera more, De Niro said he thought Scorsese might indeed want to try something a little different. "If I ever directed a movie and I wanted him for one of the main parts, he would do it," De Niro says. "I know he would do it."

In his early days, De Niro didn't choose his roles —they chose him. He was made certain offers and he was lucky to get a job. He had leads in movies like *Sam's Song,* and he also had small parts in others— roles he took because a director came along with whom he wanted to work, or simply because he believed in a project. With his rise to stardom, his criteria for choosing a role changed. Chief among the things he looks for before he'll become involved with a film is a good script. He also feels it is important that the movie is cast well. "If you don't have anything that's interesting to watch," he told *American Film,* ". . . that's real or that grabs you, whether it be actors or real people, then no matter how beautiful the photography is or how great the editing, it's not going to make any difference. Like the Abscam tapes. All this blurry videotape stuff, but you're curious because of what it is. You watch it because you know a real thing is going on there."

Robert De Niro has brought to the screen a broad range of characters and a poetic vulnerability to even the most unattractive of roles he has played. A scavenger of personality in humanity's thrift shops, he is equally adept at characterizing those who would be most at home in a pair of Gucci shoes. His larger-than-life persona is perhaps a result of being so identified with the myriad performances he has given. Just as those who inhabit our dreams are actually reflections of ourselves, traces of the "real" Robert De Niro are surely to be found amidst the celluloid dreamscapes of Bruce Pearson, Vito Corleone, Travis Bickle, Michael Vronsky, Frank Raftis, et al. They are all hand-crafted gems, not one like the other, all representing one man's commitment to his craft and, by quirk of nature, its intersection with a generation's search for moral identity. Sociologists can talk about the importance of being Robert De Niro, but his films, after all, will be immortal. You know De Niro. He's the one who fills other people's bodies, who needs to fill empty vessels. He's the kid from Little Italy who won a shelfful of movie awards and Oscars. The one to whom Harvard University once awarded its Hasty Pudding Club gold pot. "I'm having a good time," he said when he got it. But knowing, from years of experience, that an empty vessel needs to be filled, he added, ". . . but I'm a little unhappy there's no pudding in this."

Postscript. Reported by movie insiders to be in production at the time of this book's publication is *The Mission*, in which De Niro will star with Jeremy Irons and Aidan Quinn. This movie is being filmed on location in the jungles of South America and is said to be based on events that took place in Paraguay more than two hundred years ago. Allegedly, the film will explore the role of the Jesuits in Paraguay in the mid-1700s.

The action of *The Mission*, in which De Niro plays a mercenary on a mission to enslave the Guarani Indians, and Jeremy Irons the head of a local Jesuit mission, begins with the signing of the Treaty of Madrid. If sources reporting on the film are accurate, De Niro's character, named Roderigo Mendoza, endures a dramatic reversal: he becomes a Jesuit and allies himself with the plight of the Guarani Indians.

Based on historical fact, *The Mission* is scheduled to release in 1987.

XVIII

Epilogue

On a chilly winter night in Manhattan's West Village, there is a long line of people stretching from the entranceway of the Eighth Street Playhouse clear to Sixth Avenue. *Once Upon a Time in America*—Sergio Leone's ethereal uncut version—has just begun a two-week engagement ("Possibly longer," the theater's manager says). It has been playing to a full house every night since it has opened. A quick glance over the faces of the faithful discerns at least one celebrity in attendance—a famous Hollywood comedian/actor, come to see his pal, whom John Belushi used to call "Bobby D." It is nearly seven-thirty, and the three-thirty showing has just ended. In deference to the exiting filmgoers, the long line of people waiting to enter the theater moves slightly toward the curb. A man of medium build, in a suede winter coat, cowboy boots and cowboy hat goes by. The coat's turned-up collar covers the man's mouth, and a pair of lightly tinted sunglasses cover his eyes. He is sized up from his boots to the famous mole just barely visible above the right cheek. In a split-second, the mysterious man in the suede winter coat acknowledges his discoverer, his quiet double-take. He nods, buries his head into his chin, and trundles off toward Sixth Avenue.

Selected Plays

Glamour, Glory and Gold by Jackie Curtis

Opened: August 7, 1968, Bastiano's Cellar Studio
Directed by: Ron Link
Starring: Candy Darling, Jean Richards, Robert De Niro
(Lincoln Center Library has no other statistics)

One Night Stands of a Noisy Passenger by Shelley
    Winters

Opened: December 30, 1970, Actors Playhouse N.Y., N.Y.
Closed: January 3, 1971, after seven performances
Directed by: Patricia Carmichael
Starring: Richard Lynch, Sally Kirkland, Elizabeth Franz,
    Sam Schacht, Diane Ladd and Robert De Niro

Kool Aid by Merle Molofsky

Opened: November 3, 1971, Repertory Theatre Company
    of Lincoln Center
Closed: November 6, 1971 after a limited engagement of
    6 performances
Directed by: Jack Gelber
Starring: Robert De Niro, Kevin O'Connor, Barbara
    eda-Young

Schubert's Last Serenade by Julie Bovasso

Opened: June 13, 1973, Manhattan Theatre Club
Closed: June 17, 1973
Directed by: Julie Bovasso
Starring: Robert De Niro, Laura Esterman, Ted Henning,
   Dan Potter

Filmography

Greetings (1968)

Director: Brian De Palma
Screenplay: Charles Hirsch
Produced by: Charles Hirsch (Sigma III)
Running Time: 88 minutes

    CAST
    Jon Rubin...................... Robert De Niro
    Paul Shaw ....Jonathan Warden
    Lloyd Clay..................... Gerritt Graham

The Wedding Party (1969)

Director: Brian De Palma
Screenplay: Brian De Palma, Cynthia Munroe, Wilfred
    Leach
Photography: Peter Powell
Music: John Herbert McDowell
Produced by: Brian De Palma, Cynthia Munroe, Wilfred
    Leach (Powell Productions and Odine
    Presentations)
Running time: 90 minutes

    CAST
    Cecil .... Robert De Niro

Bridegroom..................... Charles Pfluger
Bride............................. Jill Clayburgh
Phoebe........................... Jennifer Salt

Hi, Mom! (1970)

Director: Brian De Palma
Screenplay: Brian De Palma, Charles Hirsch
Photography: Robert Elfstrom
Music: Eric Kaz
Produced by: Charles Hirsch (Sigma III)

CAST
Jon Rubin...................... Robert De Niro
Joe Banner........................ Allen Garfield
Judy Bishop....................... Jennifer Salt
Gerrit Wood .... Gerritt Graham

Bloody Mama (1970)

Director: Roger Corman
Screenplay: Robert Thom/Don Peters
Photography: John Alonzo
Music: Don Randi
Produced by: Roger Corman (American International
    Pictures)

CAST
Kate (Ma) Barker................ Shelley Winters
Herman Barker .... Don Stroud
Arthur Barker.................. Clint Kimbrough
Lloyd Barker.................... Robert De Niro
Sam Pendlebury..................... Pat Hingle

Born to Win (1971)

Director: Ivan Passer
Screenplay: David Scott Milton
Photography: Jack Priestly, Richard Kratina
Produced by: Philip Langer (United Artists)
Running time: 90 minutes

> CAST
> J.................................. George Segal
> Veronica.......................... Paula Prentiss
> Parm.............................. Karen Black
> Billy Dynamite.................... Jay Fletcher
> The Geek.......................... Hector Elizondo
> Danny............................. Robert De Niro

The Gang That Couldn't Shoot Straight (1971)

Director: James Goldstone
Screenplay: Waldo Salt
Story: Based on the novel by Jimmy Breslin
Photography: Owen Roizman
Music: Dave Grusin
Produced by: Robert Chartoff and Irwin Winkler
   (M.G.M.)

> CAST
> Kid Sally......................... Jerry Orbach
> Angela .... Leigh Taylor-Young
> Big Momma......................... Jo Van Fleet
> Mario .... Robert De Niro
> Baccala........................... Lionel Stander

Jennifer on My Mind (1971)

Director: Noel Black
Screenplay: Erich Segal
Story: Based on the novel *Heir* by Roger L. Simon
Music: Stephen J. Lawrence
Produced by: Bernard Schwarta (United Artists)
Running time: 90 minutes

> CAST
> Marcus .... Michael Brandon
> Jenny............................ Tippy Walker
> Max .... Lou Gilbert
> Ornstein .... Steve Vinovich and Robert De Niro

Sam's Song (1971)

Director: Jordan Leondopoulos
Photography: Alex Phillips, Jr.
Edited by: Arline Garson
Music: Gershon Kingsley
Produced by: Christopher C. Dewey (Canon Releasing
    Corp.)
Running time: 120 minutes

> CAST
> Sam .... Robert De Niro
> Andrew .... Jarred Mickey
> Erica .... Jennifer Warren
> Carol .... Terrayne Crawford
> Girl With the Hourglass.................... Viva

Bang the Drum Slowly (1973)

Director: John Hancock
Screenplay: Mark Harris
Story: Based on the novel by Mark Harris
Photography: Richard Shore
Edited by: Richard Marks
Music: Stephen Lawrence
Produced by: Maurice and Lois Rosenfeld
Running time: 98 minutes

CAST
Bruce Pearson .... Robert De Niro
Henry Wiggen .... Michael Moriarty
Dutch Schnell................. Vincent Gardenia
Joe Jaros........................... Phil Foster
Katie........................ Ann Wedgeworth

AWARD: New York Film Critics Award Best Actor

Mean Streets (1973)

Director: Martin Scorsese
Screenplay: Martin Scorsese, Mardik Martin
Photography: Kent Wakeford
Music: The Rolling Stones; The Chantells; Giuseppe de
      Stephano; Renato Carosone; The Marvelettes; Eric
      Clapton; The Miracles, et al.
Produced by: Jonathan T. Taplin (Warner Brothers)
Running time: 110 minutes

CAST
Charlie .... Harvey Keitel
Johnny Boy .... Robert De Niro
Teresa........................... Amy Robinson
Michael........................ Richard Romanns

AWARD: National Society of Film Critics, New York Film
Critics Circle Best Supporting Actor

The Godfather, Part II (1974)

Director: Francis Ford Coppola
Screenplay: Francis Ford Coppola, Mario Puzo
Photography: Gordon Willis
Edited by: Peter Zinner, Barry Malkin, Richard Marks
Music: Carmine Coppola, Nino Rota
Produced by: Francis Ford Coppola (Paramount)
Running time: 200 minutes

> CAST
> Vito Corleone................... Robert De Niro
> Michael Corleone...................... Al Pacino
> Tom Hagen...................... Robert Duvall
> Fredo Corleone .... John Cazale
> Frankie Pentangeli .... Michael V. Gazzo
> Kay .... Diane Keaton
> Hyman Roth...................... Lee Strasberg
> Sonny .... James Caan

AWARD: Academy Award, Best Supporting Actor

Taxi Driver (1976)

Director: Martin Scorsese
Screenplay: Paul Schrader
Photography: Michael Chapman
Edited by: Tom Rolf, Melvin Shapiro
Produced by: Michael and Julia Phillips (Columbia
Pictures)
Running time: 112 minutes

CAST
Travis Bickle.................... Robert De Niro
Iris............................... Jodie Foster
Sport............................. Harvey Keitel
Betsy........................... Cybill Shepherd
Wizard .... Peter Boyle
Charles Palantine................ Leonard Harris

The Last Tycoon (1976)

Director: Elia Kazan
Screenplay: Harold Pinter
Story: Based on the unfinished novel by F. Scott
    Fitzgerald
Photography: Victor Kemper
Edited by: Richard Marks
Music: Maurice Jarre
Produced by: Sam Spiegel (Paramount)
Running time: 125 minutes

CAST
Monroe Stahr .... Robert De Niro
Pat Brady...................... Robert Mitchum
Rodriguez .... Tony Curtis
Brimmer .... Jack Nicholson
Kathleen Moore................. Ingrid Boulting

1900 (1977)

Director: Bernardo Bertolucci
Screenplay: Bernardo Bertolucci, Franco Arcalli, Giuseppe
    Bertolucci
Photography: Vittorio Storaro
Edited by: Franco Arcalli

Music: Ennio Morricone
Produced by: Alberto Grimaldi (Paramount)
Running time: 245 minutes

CAST

Alfredo	Robert De Niro
Olmo	Gerard Depardieu
Attila	Donald Sutherland
Alfredo	Burt Lancaster
Elonora	Anna-Maria Gherardi
Regina	Laura Betti

New York, New York (1977)

Director: Martin Scorsese
Screenplay: Earl Mac Rauch, Mardik Martin
Photography: Laszlo Kovacs
Music: John Kander, Fred Ebb
Produced by: Irwin Winkler, Robert Chartoff
Running time: 153 minutes

CAST

Jimmy Doyle	Robert De Niro
Francine Evans	Liza Minnelli
Tony Harwell	Lionel Stander
Paul Wilson	Barry Primus
Bernice	Mary Kay Place
Frankie Hart	Georgie Auld

The Deer Hunter (1978)

Director: Michael Cimino
Screenplay: Deric Washburn
Story: Michael Cimino, Deric Washburn, Louis Garfinkle,
   Quinn K. Redeker

Photography: Vilmos Zsigmond
Edited by: Peter Zinner
Music: Stanley Myers
Produced by: Barry Spikings, Michael Deeley, Michael
    Cimino, John Peverall (Universal Studios)
Running time: 183 minutes

    CAST
    Michael Vronsky .... Robert De Niro
    Nick........................ Christopher Walken
    Steven............................ John Savage
    Linda .... Meryl Streep
    Axel........................ Chuck Aspegren
    Stan.............................. John Cazale
    John......................... George Dzundza

Raging Bull (1980)

Director: Martin Scorsese
Screenplay: Paul Schrader, Mardik Martin
Story: Based on the book by Jake La Motta, Joseph Carter
    and Peter Savage
Photography: Michael Chapman
Edited by: Thelma Schoonmaker
Produced by: Irwin Winkler, Robert Chartoff
Running time: 128 minutes

    CAST
    Jake La Motta.................... Robert De Niro
    Vickie La Motta................. Cathy Moriarty
    Joey La Motta........................ Joe Pesci

AWARDS: Oscar 1980, Best Actor: Robert De Niro

True Confessions (1982)

Director: Ulu Grosbard
Screenplay: John Gregory Dunne, Joan Didion
Story: Based on the novel by John Gregory Dunne
Photography: Owen Roizman
Edited by: Lynzee Klingman
Music: George Delerue
Produced by: Irwin Winkler, Robert Chartoff
Running time: 110 minutes

CAST

Desmond Spellacy . . . . Robert De Niro
Tom Spellacy . . . . Robert Duvall
Jack Amsterdam . . . . Charles Durning
Brenda Samuels . . . . Rose Gregario
Seamus Fargo . . . . Burgess Meredith
Dan T. Campion . . . . Ed Flanders
Cardinal Danaher . . . . Cyril Cusack

The King of Comedy (1983)

Director: Martin Scorsese
Screenplay: Paul Zimmerman
Photography: Fred Schuler
Edited by: Thelma Schoonmaker
Music: produced by Robbie Robertson
Produced by: Arnon Milchan
Running time: 108 minutes

CAST

Rupert Pupkin . . . . Robert De Niro
Jerry Langford . . . . Jerry Lewis
Masha . . . . Sandra Bernhard
Cathy Long . . . . Shelley Hack

Rita .... Diahnne Abbott
Rupert's mother.............. Catherine Scorsese

Once Upon a Time in America (1984)

Director: Sergio Leone
Screenplay: Leonardo Benvenuti, Piero de Bernardo,
    Enrico Medioli, Franco Arcalli, Franco Ferrini,
    Sergio Leone
Story: Based on the novel *The Hoods* by Harry
    Grey
Photography: Tonio Delli Colli
Edited by: Nino Morricone
Music: Ennio Morricone
Produced by: Arnon Milchan (Ladd company/Warner
    Brothers)
Running time: 218 minutes

CAST
Noodles Aaronson .... Robert De Niro
Max............................... James Woods
Carol............................. Tuesday Weld
Deborah................... Elizabeth McGovern
Fat Moe .... Larry Rapp
Jimmy O'Donnell................. Treat Williams
Joe................................. Burt Young
Frankie............................... Joe Pesci
Police Commissioner............... Danny Aiello
Cockeye...................... William Forsythe
Patsy............................. James Hayden

Falling in Love (1984)

Director: Ulu Grosbard
Screenplay: Michael Cristofer
Photographer: Peter Suschitzky
Edited by: Michael Kahn
Music: Dave Grusin
Produced by: Marvin Worth
Running time: 106 minutes

CAST

Frank Raftis	Robert De Niro
Molly Gilmore	Meryl Streep
Ed Lasky	Harvey Keitel
Ann Raftis	Jane Kaczmarek
Brian Gilmore	David Clennon
Isabelle	Dianne Wiest

Brazil

To be released in the United States in 1986.

The Mission

Still in production; projected release in 1987.

Starring: Robert De Niro, Jeremy Irons, and Aidan Quinn
Director: Roland Joffe
Screenplay: Robert Bolt
Executive Producer: David Putnam
Producer: Fernando Ghia

DATE DUE